LANDING A LAW
ENFORCEMENT JOB

Other books by Neal Trautman:

Law Enforcement Training
Law Enforcement In-service Training Program
Law Enforcement—The Making of A Profession
A Study of Law Enforcement
How to Protect Your Kids From Internet Predators
The Cutting Edge of Police Integrity
How To Be a Great Cop

LANDING A LAW ENFORCEMENT JOB

Neal E. Trautman

Upper Saddle River, New Jersey 07458

Library of Congress Catalog-in-Publication Data

Trautman, Neal E.
    Landing a law enforcement job / by Neal E. Trautman
        p. cm.
    Includes index.
    ISBN 0-13-032530-9
    1. Law enforcement—Vocational guidance. 2. Police—Vocational guidance. 3. Job
hunting. I. Title.

HV8143 .T7253 2002
363.2'023'73—dc21   00-064256

Publisher: Jeff Johnston
Senior Acquisitions Editor: Kim Davies
Production Editor: Lori Dalberg, Carlisle Publishers Services
Production Liaison: Barbara Marttine Cappuccio
Director of Manufacturing and Production: Bruce Johnson
Managing Editor: Mary Carnis
Art Director: Marianne Frasco
Cover Design Coordinator: Miguel Ortiz
Cover Design: Lorraine Castellano
Cover Photo: © Tracey L. Williams/Williams Stock Images. Courtesy Somerset County
    Police Academy, Dr. Richard Celeste, Deputy Chief, Academy Director
Editorial Assistant: Sarah Holle
Composition: Carlisle Communications, Ltd.
Printing and Binding: Banta Harrisonburg

Prentice-Hall International (UK) Limited, *London*
Prentice-Hall of Australia Pty. Limited, *Sydney*
Prentice-Hall Canada Inc., *Toronto*
Prentice-Hall Hispanoamericana, S.A., *Mexico*
Prentice-Hall of India Private Limited, *New Delhi*
Prentice-Hall of Japan, Inc., *Tokyo*
Prentice-Hall Singapore Pte. Ltd.
Editora Prentice-Hall do Brasil, Ltda., *Rio de Janeiro*

10 9 8 7 6 5 4 3 2 1
ISBN 0-13-032530-9

Dedicated to my daughter

Heather

Abraham Lincoln was raised in poverty.

*Franklin Roosevelt was brutally struck
down with childhood polio.*

*An elementary school teacher told
Albert Einstein he was "retarded."
and humiliated him.*

*Glenn Cunningham, who broke the world
record in the one-mile run,
was told by doctors
he would never walk again
when he was a child.*

*We are only limited
by our desire and perseverance.*

CONTENTS

INTRODUCTION

The rewards of a law enforcement career are immeasurable. Yet, like most great things, the path to becoming an officer is often difficult.

The fact that you have made a commitment to improve your skills and learn new test-taking strategies speaks for itself. It shows a strong desire to be better than the rest. It indicates that you are not afraid of working hard in the pursuit of a worthy goal.

Few important achievements are reached without hard work. All of us want to make the most of our lives. You have decided to dedicate your professional life to law enforcement; a very wise and honorable decision. Now, it is time to forge forward with all the determination and guts you possess. For make no mistake about it, many long, tiring hours of study and preparation await you.

All difficult undertakings become easier when they are effectively organized. This is why *Landing a Law Enforcement Job* was written. Although hard work is necessary to be adequately prepared for employment testing, it is possible to work extremely hard without ever becoming ready. This twenty-step plan can make all the difference between success and failure. By using the materials in the workbook, your efforts will stay focused and coordinated. Your hard work will reap great results.

This book contains practical, time-proven actions that teach the skills, know-ledge, and abilities required to excel during law enforcement exams and oral boards. This is a text that provides much more than merely reading materials. The plan for your success demands your involvement. This book, and the plan that it furnishes, has been systematically developed and presented in an order that ensures your skills will complement each other.

Get ready to list your goals, complete worksheets, master special strategies and carry out actions lists. Never miss a day, for each assignment is crucial to your skill-building process. Always follow the format and complete the required tasks. After you have become an officer, be certain to use these same skills and abilities throughout your career. Most important, be a great cop. Go out and make a little history.

"The credit goes to the person who is actually in the arena; whose face is marred with the dust and sweat and blood; who knows great enthusiasm and joys. Who spends himself in the worthy cause and whose place shall never be with those weak and timid souls who knew neither victory nor defeat."

                                                                    -Teddy Roosevelt

A Final Thought before You Begin

Being a law enforcement officer is a tough, demanding job. Almost every aspect of policing calls for discipline. Staying in good physical condition, knowing the facts of a case before you testify, conducting aggressive patrol on midnight shift, dealing with the frustration of the judicial system, and not letting the sarcasm of a street punk get to you are all good examples. Everything takes discipline.

To some people, discipline only means hard work or punishment. They envision having to do things they don't want to do, or not being able to do what they want. It is safe to conclude that they have never experienced the rewards that self-discipline has to offer.

Disciplined individuals are more satisfied with themselves. They don't cringe at the thought of self-control because the benefits are more than worth the effort. They are happier, have a healthier self-image and look forward to the future.

You can't feel good about your job and the work you do unless you like yourself. If you aren't disciplined, the first step is to make a sincere commitment to improve. Few things in life are more satisfying than the feeling that comes from accomplishment.

Those who achieve the most are always disciplined. Don't procrastinate. Start now and make discipline an every day habit.

It is my hope that this twenty-step planner will enhance your self-control and perseverance by providing you with regular assignments to complete. Make a sincere personal pledge right now to complete each exercise in the time and manner specified. This is just as important to landing a law enforcement job as anything that could be done.

Get discipline; every great cop has it!

Good luck,

Neal E. Trautman

ABOUT THE AUTHOR

Mr. Trautman was a founder of the Law Enforcement Training Network (LETN), the world's largest provider of police training. As the network's Director of Training, he was responsible for all aspects of training provided to 120,000 officers daily. He completed his doctoral dissertation on the Code of Silence.

During his sixteen year "sworn" police career, he was awarded

- Decorations of Heroism, 1974 and 1985
- Officer of the Year, 1976
- Police Excellence Award, 1978
- Nominated National Officer of the Year, 1980
- Runner Up, County Officer of the Year, 1981
- Meritorious Police Duty Medal, 1986

Professional Achievements

Author of nine published textbooks

Executive Director, National Institute of Ethics

President, International Association of Ethics Trainers

Currently on the Board of Directors, American Academy of Police Psychology

Past Chair, International Association of Chiefs of Police, Ad Hoc Ethics Training SubCommittee

Past Chair, American Society of Law Enforcement Trainers, Ethics Committee

Past Co-Chair, International Association of Chiefs of Police, Police Image and Ethics Committee

Past Chair, American Society of Law Enforcement Trainers, Professional Development Committee

Previously on the Board of Directors, Ethics in the Public Service, International Network

STEP

"A law enforcement career gives you the satisfaction of knowing the lives of some people are a little better because you were there when they needed help."

—Neal Trautman

SAMPLE STEP

Below is an example of the daily guides you will find in this book.

DATE: Write in date.

OBJECTIVE:

States what you will accomplish by finishing the day's assignment.

PURPOSE:

Explains the importance of the day's assignments in your journey toward achieving a career in law enforcement.

TIME REQUIRED: An estimate of the time you will need to complete the assignments.

ASSIGNMENTS:

Describes the specific tasks you must complete in order to achieve the day's objective.

QUESTIONS • COMMENTS • THINGS TO DO

This space is to be used for any notes you care to make regarding the day's assignments or things you wish to do in the future.

"Training is everything. The peach was once a bitter almond; cauliflower is nothing but cabbage with a college education."

—Mark Twain

ATTITUDE IS EVERYTHING—CHECK YOURS

DATE:

OBJECTIVE:

To eliminate all negativity from your thinking. You will learn how to allow only positive, encouraging thoughts to guide your future.

PURPOSE:

Negative thinking can be a self-fulfilling prophecy. When you begin to doubt your ability to achieve your goals in life, you may find you lack the courage to continue the journey toward those goals. If you maintain a confident, optimistic outlook, however, you will be able to keep going in the face of any adversity and overcome all your obstacles one by one.

By showing you how to keep a positive attitude in any circumstance, today's assignments will enable you to keep going when the going gets tough.

TIME REQUIRED: Three hours.

ASSIGNMENTS:

1. Study the chapter titled "What Makes a Great Cop," in *How To Be A Great Cop,* by Neal E. Trautman. (Prentice Hall)
2. List the ten most valuable things in your life.
3. List the three best things that have ever happened to you and briefly describe how each made you feel.
4. Briefly explain, in writing, why a positive attitude is crucial to attaining a career in law enforcement.

5. Have three friends write letters of recommendation for you. Besides being important components of a strong job application, such letters will serve to boost your confidence if you begin to waver in your resolve. Don't hesitate to re-read the kind words of your friends as often as necessary.

THE TEN MOST VALUABLE THINGS IN MY LIFE:

1. _____
   _____
   _____

2. _____
   _____
   _____

3. _____
   _____
   _____

4. _____
   _____
   _____

5. _____
   _____
   _____

6. _____
   _____
   _____

7. _____
   _____
   _____

8. _____
   _____
   _____

9. _____
   _____
   _____

10. _____
    _____
    _____

Reviewing the above list will help remind you that there are things worth striving for, no matter what the cost or effort involved. Refer to this list whenever you begin to feel that perhaps obtaining a career in law enforcement just isn't worth the effort involved. It is.

THE THREE BEST THINGS THAT EVER HAPPENED TO ME AND HOW THEY MADE ME FEEL:

1. _____
   _____
   _____
   _____

2. _____
   _____
   _____
   _____

3. _____
   _____
   _____
   _____

Review the above list when you feel down or discouraged. Recalling times when you felt most positive and good about yourself will help overcome any doubts about your abilities or skills that might creep into your mind.

WHY A POSITIVE ATTITUDE IS CRUCIAL TO MY ATTAINING A CAREER IN LAW ENFORCEMENT:

_____
_____
_____
_____
_____
_____
_____
_____

If you begin to feel that you are merely going through the motions of the exercises in this book without enthusiasm or attention, re-read what you have written above. If you don't put your heart into what you are doing as you prepare for your law enforcement career, you won't get the results you want. **Be passionate!**

Never allow yourself to forget, even for a moment, the drive and desire you feel at this moment. Refuse to be denied!

QUESTIONS • COMMENTS • THINGS TO DO

Check with your local agencies to see if you can become a police explorer. It's a great way to get an "edge" on other applicants.

STEP

2

"Nothing great will ever be achieved without great men, and men are great only if they are determined to be so."

—**Charles de Gaulle**

DREAMS, GOALS, SKILLS, AND ACHIEVEMENTS

DATE:

OBJECTIVE:

To define your dreams, goals, skills, and achievements.

PURPOSE:

Because many of our goals arise from dreams of what we would like to be or accomplish in life, you will first create a dreams list. Although a certain dream may seem totally out of reach, by writing it down you give it a power that it would never have in your mind.

Goals are crucial to your success. Living without goals is like driving without a map—you'll get somewhere, but it may not be the place you intended, and you will experience plenty of frustration along the way. It is essential that you develop your own written, personalized set of goals. By consciously deciding where you want to go in life, you will dramatically increase your chances of reaching your destination.

Finally, taking time to think through and list your skills and achievements will ensure that you have these facts firmly in mind when you are being interviewed, and will give you the confidence that comes from knowing you have what it takes!

TIME REQUIRED: Three hours.

ASSIGNMENTS:

1. Create your dream list. Write down anything that comes to mind, no matter how outrageous. You'll find that as you write down dreams, more and more will come to mind.

2. Create your goal list.
3. List your skills.
4. List your achievements.
5. Preparation task: Subscribe to one or more police magazines.

Note: Although not required in this assignment, it is strongly suggested that you have your spouse fill out his or her dreams and goals lists as well.

MY DREAMS LIST

With unlimited ability, money, self-confidence, and knowledge, this is what I would have, do, and become:

1. _____
   _____
2. _____
   _____
3. _____
   _____
4. _____
   _____
5. _____
   _____
6. _____
   _____
7. _____
   _____
8. _____
   _____
9. _____
   _____
10. _____
    _____
11. _____
    _____
12. _____
    _____
13. _____
    _____

14. _____
   _____
15. _____
   _____

Make as many copies of this page as you need.

Be sure you make your goals realistic and specific. For instance, if one of your goals is to lose weight, state precisely how much weight you want to lose and by what date. The more specific your goals, the more likely you are to achieve them. Make sure many of the goals you list today concern your commitment to prepare for your written exam and oral board. Specify timetables and levels of achievement.

MY GOALS LIST—PROFESSIONAL

1. _____
2. _____
3. _____
4. _____
5. _____
6. _____
7. _____
8. _____
9. _____
10. _____

MY GOALS LIST—PERSONAL

1. _____
2. _____
3. _____
4. _____
5. _____
6. _____
7. _____
8. _____
9. _____
10. _____

Make as many copies of this page as you need.

MY SKILLS LIST

List ten skills you possess that might be useful to a law enforcement agency and that could be mentioned during an oral board or interview. Fill out the full list of ten skills, no matter how irrelevant some might seem. It is impossible to predict what skills a potential employer will require. Your unusual abilities may provide just the edge you need to get the job.

You will find it very useful to memorize this list; you will not be able to refer to it during job interviews and oral boards.

1. _____
2. _____
3. _____
4. _____
5. _____
6. _____
7. _____
8. _____
9. _____
10. _____

MY ACHIEVEMENTS LIST

List ten personal or professional achievements that may be useful to mention during an oral board or job interview. You are more likely to be hired if you can tell an interviewer about specific accomplishments in your past jobs. Again, memorizing the list is important.

1. _____
2. _____
3. _____
4. _____
5. _____
6. _____
7. _____
8. _____
9. _____
10. _____

Learn more about law enforcement by subscribing to one or more of the following excellent magazines. The knowledge you will gain will help during interviews and oral boards.

- *Law and Order* is published monthly by Hendon, Inc., 1000 Skokie Blvd., Wilmette, IL 60091. Phone (708) 256-8555. $17 per year.
- *Police Chief* is published monthly by the International Association of Chiefs of Police, 1110 North Glebe Road, Suite 200, Arlington, VA 22201. Phone (800) 843-4227. $25 per year.
- *Police* is published monthly by Hare Publications, 6300 Yarrow Drive, Carlsbad, CA 92009-1596. Phone (800) 854-6449. $18.95 per year.

You will find information about some other law enforcement publications in the Appendix.

QUESTIONS • COMMENTS • THINGS TO DO

STEP
3

Make a Commitment to Master Your Fears and The Application Process

DATE:

OBJECTIVE:

To prevent anxiety by learning the four main reasons people don't get hired and to make a written commitment to study for your law enforcement exam.

PURPOSE:

Negative thinking is one of the main reasons people don't achieve their goals in life. Fear is one form of negative thinking that affects everyone from time to time. Today you will focus on conquering one specific fear—the fear that you will not succeed in your quest for a law enforcement career. By learning the four main reasons people don't get hired, you will be prepared to avoid these traps and thus drastically reduce any anxiety you may be feeling.

Second, you will make a commitment to study effectively and list any bad study habits you intend to eliminate. As discussed in Step 2, written goals have many times the power of those held only in your mind. By thinking through and writing down your negative study habits, you will be in a much better position to conquer those bad habits.

TIME REQUIRED: Three hours.

ASSIGNMENTS:

1. Read the text titled "The Four Main Reasons People Don't Get Hired."
2. List your fears about the police hiring process and explain how you will overcome those fears.
3. Write a paragraph making a commitment to study effectively.
4. List negative study habits you will overcome and how you will overcome them.

THE FOUR MAIN REASONS PEOPLE DON'T GET HIRED

The sheer size of America's law enforcement system is astonishing. More than 15,000 agencies across the country offer approximately 600,000 jobs, making law enforcement a very large employer. In addition to its size, the police force is unmatched in benefits and working conditions. Law enforcement can be the greatest career in the world, if you have what it takes.

In fact, hundreds of thousands of people are beginning to realize just how great a career in law enforcement can be. More and more people just like yourself want to become part of the best organization in the country.

Of course, this means that law enforcement agencies everywhere are being flooded with applications, and the agencies can afford to be choosy about who they accept. Each agency will do everything in its power to weed out all but the best of the best.

Can you make it all the way? Statistics say you won't. But by knowing what to expect and what common traps you need to avoid, you can place yourself head and shoulders above the other applicants and drastically increase your chances of being hired. Prepare to meet the challenge!

The four main reasons people don't get hired by law enforcement agencies:	1. They apply at agencies where there aren't very many openings, or they don't know all the places they can apply.
	2. They don't know how to submit an application that sets them apart from the rest of the crowd.
	3. They don't know the secrets, strategies, and techniques for making the highest possible score on the written exam.
	4. They are not psychologically prepared to get through the oral board, so they don't do well.

You can overcome the first problem simply by taking the time to find out which agencies are hiring and by submitting applications to a large number of agencies. If you really want a career in law enforcement, don't limit yourself to one or two agencies—apply to at least thirty different ones. There may not be thirty agencies in your area, but if getting into one of them requires relocating to another city for a year or two, don't hesitate. Remember, getting in is the hardest part. Once you have experience, you'll have a much easier time getting a job with the agency of your choice.

Even more common than applying to too few agencies is submitting a poorly prepared application. It is essential that your job application reflects a polished, professional image and that it stands out above any other applications received by the agency. Following the guidelines presented here will ensure that your application gets a second look.

1. **Always type your application.** Many people hand-write their applications. The fact that you took the time to type yours will show that you have a higher level of professionalism than the other applicants— just what a potential employer is looking for.

2. **Prepare typed attachments** for the application areas of work history, education, and residence history. Instead of filling out these areas of the application, write "See attached," placing each attachment behind the appropriate page of the application. It will take you far less time to complete the application than if you fill each one out separately, yet the application will be completely professional in appearance.

3. **Submit all paperwork for which agencies would eventually ask along with your application.** The thickness of your application will automatically set you apart from the other applicants and make you appear more qualified, even though you've simply included documents other applicants would have been asked to provide eventually. The paperwork that agencies usually want includes copies of your birth certificate, high school diploma, social security card, and DD214 form if you were in the military. Also include letters of recommendation and any other paperwork that demonstrates your abilities. After you have assembled these documents for your first application, make twenty or thirty copies so you can easily attach them to future applications without any extra effort.

4. **Prepare a high-quality résumé and cover letter to submit with your application.** If you've never prepared a résumé before, there are several easy ways to go about it. Buy a book on résumé preparation

or check one out of your local library and follow their tried-and-true formats, inserting your own personal information. Or have a résumé service prepare one for you. These services are inexpensive, and the Yellow Pages, newspapers, and bulletin boards at any college have many listings. Résumé-preparation books usually contain sample cover letters as well. Using the book's format, type your own cover letter. You may also use the sample cover letter included at the end of today's assignments. You can use the same text for each application, so the effort involved is minimal—but the image you present is exceptional. Lastly, make sure you use high-quality paper for your résumé, cover letter, and application attachments. Using colored paper is another way to set your application apart from the crowd, but be conservative in your choice of colors. Cream and gray are always good, safe choices.

> Problems three and four—not being adequately prepared for your written exam and oral board—are more complicated. You will need to study to be successful in these areas. The bulk of this book is concerned with preparing you for these exams, and strategies to help you pass with flying colors will be addressed in future assignments.

FEARS CONCERNING THE LAW ENFORCEMENT HIRING PROCESS

The law enforcement hiring process is complex and difficult. Because you're probably unfamiliar with the testing procedures that lie ahead, they may seem frightening. Fear of the unknown is natural, but you don't have to let it control or depress you. List below your fears concerning the hiring process, and state how you will overcome each fear.

1. _____

I will overcome this fear by _____

2. _____

I will overcome this fear by _____

3. _____

I will overcome this fear by _____

4. _____

I will overcome this fear by _____

COMMITMENT TO STUDY EFFECTIVELY

I, _____, make a personal commitment to study effectively by doing the following:

_____

_____

_____

_____

Following is a list of poor study habits I have had in the past. I will not continue them.

1. _____
2. _____
3. _____
4. _____
5. _____

Here is an example of a concise, yet powerful, cover letter. You can use it when applying to any agency by simply changing the address, or you may wish to use a more detailed cover letter.

June 1, 2001

Lt. John E. Smith
Big Police Department
1234 East Main Street
Major City, Large State 99999

Dear Lt. Smith:

Please accept the attached resume as an overview of my professional qualifications.

Although this application is comprehensive, it cannot convey the high level of my performance. I am a dedicated and hard worker with exceptional communication skills and unique abilities. I would deeply appreciate the opportunity to serve your police department as an officer.

My telephone number is (000) 555-5555. I look forward to hearing from you.

Sincerely,

Job Hunter

QUESTIONS • COMMENTS • THINGS TO DO

If you live in an area close to a university or college, check to see if they have a criminal justice or law enforcement club or fraternity.

STEP 4

"Choose a job you love, and you will never have to work a day in your life."

—Confucius

HIRING REQUIREMENTS AND ORGANIZING AGENCY PHONE NUMBERS

DATE:

OBJECTIVE:

To become very familiar with the basic qualifications you will need in order to be hired as a law enforcement officer, and to start a list of phone numbers of agencies in your area.

PURPOSE:

You can save a lot of time and aggravation by understanding the basic requirements for being considered for a career in law enforcement. If you don't meet all the requirements now, you can take steps to become qualified before you spend unnecessary time and effort looking for a police job.

Listing agency phone numbers will serve a double purpose. It will familiarize you with the law enforcement agencies in your area and prepare you to contact these agencies a little further down the road.

TIME REQUIRED: 90 minutes.

ASSIGNMENTS:

1. Study the section titled "Basic Qualifications" and determine how to correct any deficiencies you may have.
2. Make a list of the phone numbers of law enforcement agencies to which you would like to apply.

BASIC REQUIREMENTS FOR GETTING A JOB IN LAW ENFORCEMENT

1. **Age Restrictions.** Most agencies specify a range of acceptable ages for candidates wishing to enter the police force. The minimum requirement varies from 19 to 21 years of age. The maximum is usually around 35 years of age. However, some departments don't have a maximum age requirement. Instead, they depend on the medical and physical fitness examinations, which tend to eliminate most candidates around that age.

2. **U.S. Citizen.** You must be a U.S. citizen to be a police officer. Sometimes you will be required to live within a specific distance of the agency to which you are applying. Don't be discouraged if you don't meet the distance requirement; you can always move.

3. **Diploma or G.E.D.** All agencies require you to have a high school diploma or G.E.D. Although few agencies require a college education, higher education will be a benefit throughout your career.

4. **Documentation.** You will need to provide an assortment of documents to the agency before you can be hired. These documents include a valid driver's license, birth certificate, high school diploma, social security card, and honorable military discharge, if applicable. As discussed earlier, you should submit photocopies of these documents with your original application. Don't wait until you're asked.

5. **Medical Exam.** This is a standard medical exam, designed to make sure you are in good health. It's no more rigorous than most pre-employment physicals, and the agency usually pays for it. Be aware that this exam does include a drug test; no one who uses illegal drugs will be considered for a law enforcement job.

6. **No Felony Conviction.** A felony conviction record usually will eliminate you immediately from consideration, as will some misdemeanors. Don't think you can get by without mentioning it if these things are on your record. The agency will check.

7. **Background Investigation.** Once you've passed your written exam with a high score, someone will be assigned to investigate your past. This is an extensive investigation designed to ensure that only the most upstanding citizens are considered for police positions, and that's as it should be. Law enforcement officers serve as examples to the rest of the nation. If you are afraid that your background won't stand up to an investigation, perhaps you should reevaluate your desire to be a police officer.

8. **Experience.** Few agencies have experience requirements for entry-level enforcement positions. It sounds too good to be true, but the fact is that many agencies actually prefer that you not have previous experience. They would rather teach you the habits they want you to have right from the beginning rather than have to train you out of old, bad habits. If you meet all the requirements above, your lack of experience should not be too great a hurdle.

Get Organized—Start Researching Your Agencies

It is crucial that you develop a system for keeping track of upcoming openings at local law enforcement agencies. Most people trying to enter the field of law enforcement never know when there's an opening. They become frustrated when they repeatedly find out about openings after they have been filled.

Another common problem is that some law enforcement agencies only accept applications during a specific, and often very brief, time period. If you miss that period, you miss the chance to be considered for any open positions.

Don't count on the agencies notifying you about application periods either through mailings or through the newspaper. They usually won't. The only way to learn about job availability at different agencies is to take the initiative to keep in touch. Make a list of agencies in your area and call them often. Not only will this keep you informed about any upcoming job openings, it will also send the clear message that you are very interested in working for them—a definite mark in your favor when the time comes to send in your application.

It's hard, frustrating work, but it will be worth it. Get organized and keep a chart showing important information about each agency.

LAW ENFORCEMENT AGENCIES

Agency   Phone Number

1. _____
2. _____
3. _____
4. _____
5. _____
6. _____
7. _____
8. _____
9. _____
10. _____
11. _____
12. _____
13. _____
14. _____
15. _____
16. _____
17. _____
18. _____
19. _____
20. _____
21. _____
22. _____
23. _____
24. _____
25. _____

QUESTIONS • COMMENTS • THINGS TO DO

"The strongest single factor in prosperity consciousness is self-esteem: believing you can do it, believing you deserve it, believing you will get it."

—Jerry Gillies

ORGANIZE YOUR STUDY TIME

DATE:

OBJECTIVE:

To get organized!

PURPOSE:

By learning to organize your study time effectively, you'll find you can learn twice as much in half the time.

TIME REQUIRED: Three hours.

ASSIGNMENTS:

1. Study the section titled "You Can Get There From Here."
2. Use the chart provided to record your study goals.
3. Fill out the Test Registration Results chart as applicable.
4. Track your organization process with the Daily Progress Report.

YOU CAN GET THERE FROM HERE

So now you're ready to start studying for that exam. But just where and how do you start? Setting goals is the key.

Developing good study skills is crucial to achieving your goals—not just your academic goals, but those involving every area of your life.

Good study skills will transfer to any preparation tasks you may need to accomplish to achieve your goals. Following are some hints that you will find helpful in making goal-setting a regular part of your life.

1. **Don't aim too high or too low.** You won't be motivated to achieve a goal if you don't really believe it's possible. On the other hand, if you set your goals too low, you won't accomplish everything you could have if you had made just a little more effort. Most important, don't be afraid to adjust your goals along the way. If your goal is to finish a task by a certain date, and it becomes evident that it's not going to happen, readjust your date. Don't give up! Remember, you never fail until you stop trying.

2. **Be realistic in your expectations.** For example, it is not reasonable to expect yourself to master electrical engineering if that is not your subject. You will only get bogged down. Instead, make it your goal to have an improved understanding of the subject.

3. **Don't be overly realistic!** Many people don't try to do things because they are too ready to believe they are impossible. There's a fine line between aiming high and trying to achieve the impossible; don't confuse the two. On the other hand, don't forget that very little is impossible if you are truly committed to achieving it.

4. **Focus your efforts on areas that offer the best possibility of success.** A taste of success will energize your efforts in other areas.

5. **Monitor your achievements and constantly set new goals.** Each time you achieve one goal, another should take its place. Sit down and say to yourself, "This is where I am. Where should I go now?" This way you will never be without a plan. It's easy to run out of goals and suddenly find you have to start all over again.

Creating a Study Environment

If you've ever tried to study in a very distracting environment, you know how difficult it is. Maybe the TV set is on, blaring your favorite show across the room; every couple of minutes you interrupt your studying to watch a little bit of the show. Maybe your neighbor is having a loud party next door. Or maybe your kids are constantly walking into the room, interrupting you. You just can't seem to muster the concentration you need to study effectively.

You need to create a study environment for yourself in which you can spend high-quality study time. You'll find that you accomplish twice as much in half the time.

In creating your study environment, there are many factors to take into account; what's right for you will be wrong for someone else. Do you know where, when, and how you study best? Consider the following factors.

- **Find a place where you study most effectively and use it.** Do you study best at home? In the library? At a friend's house? Somewhere else?

- **Set aside your most productive time each day for studying.** At what time of day do you study most effectively? Some people love to burn the midnight oil, while others can't keep their eyes open after 10 P.M.

- **Determine what noise level you can tolerate while studying.** Do you study best in complete quiet, with music, in front of the TV? What kind of music, what kind of TV shows?

- **Determine whether you prefer to start with the hard assignments or the easy assignments.** Some people like to tackle the tough stuff first, while they're fresh; and others prefer to warm up with the easy tasks. Plan your study time according to what works for you.

- **Plan break time into your study periods.** Remember, there's nothing wrong with taking breaks to keep yourself sharp, but they shouldn't come every five minutes! Try to increase your concentration so that you can study for an hour without a break.

- **Most people find it helpful to set up a study schedule.** However, don't be afraid to deviate from your schedule if you get bogged down or just need a break from one subject.

- **Determine whether you study best on a full or an empty stomach.** If being hungry interferes with your concentration, make sure you eat first!

By putting together the answers to these questions, you will have made a great start on creating your ideal study environment. There are no right or wrong answers; your goal is to find what works best for you. You may find different environments work for different kinds of studying. For instance, you may need complete silence for memorizing, but you may like to listen to the radio while reading or taking notes. If you have no idea what works best for you, take a week and try every method you can think of. Then use what works best. Once you've identified what works for you, avoid situations in which you don't perform your best.

Study Tips

1. **Be reasonable.** Don't try to do too much; cramming should be avoided at all costs. On the other hand, don't do too little. Strike an appropriate balance.

2. **Be realistic.** Plan your study time according to your schedule, goals, and aptitudes—not some outside standard. Don't worry about how long other people think something should take you. Some things will be easy for you and you'll accomplish them much more quickly than expected, while others will take you longer.

3. **Set priorities.** Some subjects will come easily to you and will require far less study time than others. Those are usually the subjects in which you are most interested. Resist the temptation to spend extra time on the enjoyable, easy subjects. It's on the tough ones that you need to put in the extra time.

4. **Be flexible.** When something comes up to interfere with your plans, be ready to adjust your study schedule accordingly.

5. **Constantly monitor your study plan and study schedule.** You may find that something in your study environment doesn't work as well as you thought it would, or you may fall behind or get ahead in your study schedule. Make any changes that are necessary. Remember, you set up your study plan; you can change it whenever you need to.

6. **Be prepared.** There is nothing more frustrating than sitting down to study and realizing you are missing the one crucial item you need to complete an assignment. If you need graph paper for tomorrow's assignment, write a note to remind yourself to have it on hand. That way you'll never be unable to complete a scheduled study session because you're missing the necessary equipment.

7. **Take outside factors into account when planning.** For example, if you plan to study at 8:00 with a friend who is always late, don't expect to start right on time. Schedule something you can do for 15 or 30 minutes, if necessary, while you wait for your friend.

8. **Try anything that may help get you organized.** You may find that color-coding your day-to-day calendar works wonders for your organization, or you may need a big wall calendar that is always right in front of you.

9. **Accomplish one task before moving on to the next one.** Most people find that to be easier and quicker than jumping from one subject to another.

10. **Don't try to remember things. Write them down.** Your mind will be less cluttered, and studying will be easier when you aren't trying to remember a lot of details about your study schedule.

11. **Don't let things that are "urgent" break up your study time.** It's easy to become distracted when the phone rings or you realize your favorite TV show is about to start. Always take a moment before you quit studying to make sure you've reached a logical stopping point. If you haven't, keep working until you do. If you must stop in the middle of a task, make a note to yourself about where you left off, if necessary. Then you can enjoy a break without worry.

12. **Be extra careful of time-consuming tasks.** Some study tasks will require extra time and effort, demanding your full attention from start to finish. Once you begin these tasks, you must complete them or you may lose your train of thought. If you know a task is of this nature, make especially sure you will not be interrupted. Go to the library, lock your door, turn off the ringer on the phone—do anything it takes to make sure you have a stretch of time in which you will not be disturbed.

13. **If you know a person who seems to study effectively, talk to him or her and compare study techniques.** You may learn something that will help you.

14. **Beware of daydreaming!** It's all too easy to let your mind drift when you sit down to hit the books. It's tough at the beginning, but once you get into the study habit, you'll find that just sitting down at your desk or table, or wherever you normally study will clear your mind and get you ready to work. Until that happens, be ready to say "no!" to everything that tempts you to drift off.

15. **Reward yourself.** For example, you might promise yourself an ice cream cone as a reward for completing a study task. Before you begin studying, define exactly what you must accomplish to receive the reward. You must be firm with yourself; if you don't successfully complete the assignment, no reward. Again, it may be tough at first, but by sticking to this regimen you'll find it will get easier.

STUDY GOALS

Immediate	Within Six Weeks	Within Three Months

- Prioritize each task.
- Cross out any steps that are not needed.
- Every month or six weeks, review and update your short-term and long-term objectives.

TEST REGISTRATION RECORDS

Department	Test Type	Date Registered	Test Date	Test Place	Register Score Position	Eligibility Expiration

DAILY PROGRESS REPORT

Task	Date	Done

Note: There will sometimes be several worksheets for a single day.

QUESTIONS • COMMENTS • THINGS TO DO

STEP 6

"The best things about the future are the memories you'll find along the way."

—**Neal Trautman**

ENHANCE TEST-TAKING TECHNIQUES AND PHONE TEN AGENCIES

DATE:

OBJECTIVE:

To enhance your studying and test-taking skills and to phone ten agencies.

PURPOSE:

Although the questions you will be asked on the written portion of the law enforcement exam are specific to the field of law enforcement, there are many general studying and test-taking techniques you can learn that will give you an edge. By studying the tips presented in this section, you will be much better prepared to do well on any test.

In this assignment, you will also phone ten agencies to begin gathering the information you will need to achieve your goal of landing a law enforcement job.

TIME REQUIRED: 90 minutes.

ASSIGNMENTS:

1. Study the section titled "Test-Taking Tips."
2. Study the section titled "Studying Tips."
3. Phone ten agencies.

TEST-TAKING TIPS

Our discussion will center on two types of questions you are likely to encounter on your written exam: true-false and multiple choice.

True-False Questions

A true-false question seems easy. After all, there are only two answers, so you have a 50% chance of being right even if you have no idea what the answer is. But be careful! True-false questions can be tricky. Following the tips below will help you avoid some common traps.

1. **Read each sentence as carefully as possible.** One word can change the entire meaning of a statement. If you are reading too quickly, you might miss an important point. Read the sentence slowly and carefully, word by word, as many times as necessary to feel certain you know what is being said. Only after you have done this should you attempt to answer the question.

2. If you find you're still unsure about whether the statement is true or false after you've followed step 1, you should answer false. **Answer true only when you are positive the statement is correct.**

3. **Be on the lookout for absolutes.** Sentences containing words such as "always," "never," "only," and "all" are usually false. Think about it. Very seldom in life does something "always" or "never" happen; there are usually exceptions.

Multiple Choice Questions

Like true-false questions, multiple choice questions can look deceptively easy. After all, the answer is there, right in front of you! But how do you find it? Study the tips below to give you an edge on every multiple choice test.

1. **Always take sample tests if you can get your hands on them.** The types of questions on the sample tests will give you an excellent idea of what the real test will be like in terms of both content and difficulty.

2. Like most tests, your police exam will be timed. **Go through and answer the easy questions first; then go back and**

work on the harder ones. This will ensure that you don't miss any easy questions at the end just because you ran out of time.

3. Even if you don't know the answer to a question, **you will usually be able to eliminate at least one or two of the choices.** If you have to guess at the answer, you'll have a much better chance of being correct if you've already ruled out some of the choices.

4. **If you are not sure of the correct answer, choose one anyway,** then mark the question so you can come back to it later if you have time. If you run out of time, at least you will have answered the question. You have **no** chance of getting the correct answer if you don't even make a guess!

5. **Follow your "gut feeling."** Don't change an answer after you've marked it unless you're positive you were wrong the first time. Your instincts will usually be correct.

6. **Watch for subtle clues in the question.** For instance, if a blank is preceded by *a,* you know the answer must start with a consonant; likewise, if *an* is the word, look for an answer beginning with a vowel.

7. **If you get stuck between two answers, the longest one is usually correct.**

8. **Avoid the "loner."** Sometimes you'll find three or four similar answers and one that bears no relation to the others. For example, look at the following four choices: A. chair; B. table; C. stool; D. dog. D is the "loner" in this case. The first three answers are all furniture, while a dog is an animal. The "loner" is probably not the answer. Be careful, though; sometimes the "loner" is the correct answer! Use this rule only when you have no idea which answer is correct.

9. If you're asked for the smallest number for something, and you're not sure of the answer, select the smallest or next-to-smallest of the number choices. If you're asked for the largest number, select the largest or next-to-largest answer. **The best answer is usually the next-to-smallest or next-to-largest answer.** For example: A. 3; B. 24; C. 1; D. 10; E. 7. If asked for the smallest number and you had no idea what the correct answer was, you would select A. 3, which is the next-to-smallest number listed. If the question asked for the largest number, you would choose D. 10, the next-to-largest choice.

10. **Grammar can be a clue to help you choose the correct answer.** Wrong answers sometimes are not grammatically consistent with the question because test makers don't pay as much attention to the wording of the incorrect answers as they do to the correct ones.

11. **Beware of general answers** such as "none of the above," "all of the above" and "cannot determine from information given." If you cannot decide between a specific answer and one of these generalities, choose the specific answer every time.

12. As in true-false tests, **absolutes are a strong indication that an answer is not correct.** Words such as "always," "never," "all," and "none" are seldom true. Avoid these answers if another choice seems to make sense.

13. **Choose between answers that mean the same thing or have opposite meanings.** When two possible answers have the opposite meaning, one of them is usually the correct answer; eliminate the other choices and decide between these two. Likewise, when two answers mean virtually the same thing, one of the pair is likely to be the correct choice.

14. **Never leave a question unanswered.** Even if there is a penalty for incorrect answers, as is the case on many tests, following the tips listed above virtually ensures that your correct guesses will far outweigh the penalty.

15. **If you're certain an answer is correct, select it and go on.** Don't second-guess yourself and look for traps; it may confuse you and cause you to switch to a wrong answer.

Remember, if you're properly prepared for your police exam, you won't need to use these techniques on most questions—only those that you aren't absolutely sure about. You'll find you know the answers immediately to most of the questions.

TEST-TAKING TIPS CHECKLIST

True-False Questions

- Read each sentence as carefully as possible.
- Answer true only when you are positive the statement is correct.
- Be on the lookout for absolutes.

Multiple Choice Questions

- Always take sample tests, if possible.
- Answer the easy questions first, then return to the hard ones.
- Eliminate one or two of the choices to increase your chances of guessing correctly.
- If you don't know an answer, choose one anyway, then mark the question and return to it later.
- Watch for subtle grammatical clues.
- Avoid the "loner."
- The longest answer is usually correct.
- The next-to-smallest or next-to-largest number is usually correct.
- Use grammar as a clue to help you choose the correct answer.
- Choose specific answers over general answers.
- Avoid absolutes.
- If two answers mean either virtually the same thing or just the opposite of each other, choose between these answers.
- Never leave a question unanswered.
- If you're certain an answer is correct, select it and go on. Don't look for traps.

STUDYING TIPS

One of the most important things to keep in mind is that effective studying requires organization! You cannot cram at the last minute for your police exam. Your mind can't take in vast quantities of information at once. To really learn a body of material, you should study for approximately 15 to 30 minutes per day for as long as it takes to get through all the information.

Set aside a specific time period each day when you will sit down to study. You may find this discipline difficult at first, but as time goes by and you continue on your program, you will be amazed at how easy the learning process is when you approach it this way.

If you're like most people, you know the words to hundreds of popular songs, even the ones you dislike, just because those songs happened to be playing in the car on your way to work. You certainly didn't make any effort to learn the words. Wouldn't it be great if all learning was that easy? It is. **Repetition is the key to the learning process.** Devote your last study session each week to a review of what you have learned during the previous six days. At the end of the second week of study, review not only that week's lessons but also those from the first week. At the end of the third week, review the first, second, and third weeks. You'll find that after three or four repetitions, the information becomes second nature—just like those pop songs you can't get out of your head. By the time the exam rolls around, you'll know the answers so well that you won't even have to think about them. And all in just 15 minutes per day!

Make a commitment right now to studying 15 to 30 minutes per day for your oral and written exams. It's a small price to pay for achieving the career of a lifetime.

QUESTIONS • COMMENTS • THINGS TO DO

PHONE TEN AGENCIES

Phone ten agencies and learn everything you can about their requirements. First ask if they will mail you a copy of their employment requirements and information about upcoming employment examinations. If they will not, ask what their employment requirements are regarding their application process, age, written examination, oral board, physical fitness test, polygraph, current openings, and upcoming openings. Record the information in the space provided below.

Agency	Application Process	Age	Physical Fitness Test	Current Openings	Written Exam	Oral Board	Notes/Other

STEP 7

"If you could sell your experience for what it cost you, you would have a fortune."

—Herbert Prochnow

MASTER POLICE PROCEDURE TEST QUESTIONS AND PHONE TEN AGENCIES

DATE:

OBJECTIVE:

To become effective in answering procedure test questions by identifying key words and understanding procedure ideas and to phone ten agencies.

PURPOSE:

By learning to answer test questions related to police procedure, you will overcome one of the obstacles in your path to a law enforcement career.

By phoning ten agencies and recording the information you receive, you will be well on your way to having the facts you need to begin your application process.

TIME REQUIRED: Three hours.

ASSIGNMENTS:

1. Read the chapter titled "Surviving the Street," in *How To Be A Great Cop.*
2. Read and study the section titled "Test-Taking Techniques."
3. Read the section titled "Drawing Conclusions" and answer test questions on procedure.
4. Phone ten agencies and record the information you receive.

TEST-TAKING TECHNIQUES

A high score on the law enforcement written exam is arguably the most important component in a successful job search. Do well on this exam and it's likely that you will find yourself wearing the badge of a law enforcement officer. But be warned—this exam is tough! It's specifically designed to weed out as many applicants as possible; only those who score at the very top of the scale will be hired.

Only a tiny percentage of those who take the law enforcement written exam without preparation will do well; most will do poorly or fail. This is a well-known fact. Yet many people, even knowing this, choose to walk into the exam without making the slightest attempt to prepare themselves. Why? Because they have no idea how to prepare! In fact, most people who take the law enforcement entrance exam don't even know that it is possible to prepare. When they get to the exam, they're blown away.

A typical entrance exam contains about 110 questions that must be answered in 65 minutes. To make matters worse, some of the questions are tricky—you must know exactly what you're up against to answer correctly. Common sense won't do it on this test.

Learning the Secrets

Afraid? Don't be. Anyone can get a high score if they know how. You've already learned some tricks that will help you do better on any exam. Starting today, you will learn specific information and techniques that will enable you to score 100% on the law enforcement exam. Don't set your sights on anything less. A score of 90% may be good, but it doesn't set you apart the way a perfect score of 100% does.

Mastering Police Procedure Questions	*There are three keys to understanding the procedure section of the police employment exam.*
	Underline the key words.
	Take time to understand the ideas in each sentence and paragraph.
	Test yourself by asking yourself questions about each procedure.

Drawing Conclusions

What evidence is needed for you to be certain a conclusion is true? Here's a sample question to help us understand. The statement in question is this: "Summary of evidence collected to date: All officers in the precinct are overweight and under 55 years of age."

A prematurely drawn conclusion would be, "Any person in the precinct who is under 55 years of age is a police officer."

Which one of the following additional pieces of evidence, if any, would make it reasonably certain that the conclusion drawn is true?

A. Each person who is under 55 years of age is overweight.
B. All persons who are overweight are under 55 years of age.
C. No one who is under 55 years of age has a vocation other than policing.
D. None of these.

The first thing you should do is underline the key words in each sentence. The "summary of evidence collected to date" is what we assume is true; all officers are overweight and under 55. The "prematurely drawn conclusion" that must be proven is that any person under 55 is a police officer.

What would make us reasonably certain that this conclusion is true? Let's examine the choices.

Underline the key words:

A. <u>Each person</u> who is <u>under 55</u> years of age is <u>overweight.</u>
B. <u>All persons</u> who are <u>overweight</u> are <u>under 55</u> years of age.
C. <u>No one</u> who is <u>under 55</u> years of age has a <u>vocation other than policing.</u>
D. None of these.

Choice C is correct. Anyone under 55 is a police officer, which is precisely what the prematurely drawn conclusion said.

Practice your new procedures test-taking skills by answering the sample test questions in the following section.

POLICE PROCEDURES SAMPLE TEST QUESTIONS

Answer questions 1 through 5 solely on the basis of the following passage. Read the passage thoroughly, then answer the questions without referring back to the passage.

Polygraph Examination

The polygraph examination is often called a lie-detector test, although it does not detect lies. It measures changes in a human being's physiological responses: pulse, blood pressure, respiration rate and volume, and changes in skin resistance. From these changes the polygraph examiner can suggest what questions triggered a peculiar response from the person being examined.

The polygraph is no longer being used as a preemployment testing device except by specially authorized agencies. Law enforcement agencies are still able to use the polygraph; convenience stores and the like are not.

The polygraph examination is allowable as an investigative aid in criminal cases if the person taking the polygraph has been advised of his or her rights and then submits to examination.

1. What is a polygraph commonly called?
   A. detection test   C. lie examination
   B. lie-detector test   D. none of the above
2. What does a polygraph measure?
   A. whether the test subject is lying C. physiological responses
   B. physical responses   D. none of the above
3. Are convenience stores able to use the polygraph as a preemployment test?
   A. yes   C. not enough information
   B. no   D. none of the above
4. Does the polygraph measure blood pressure?
   A. yes   C. not enough information
   B. no   D. none of the above
5. Is it illegal to use the polygraph in criminal investigations?
   A. yes   C. not enough information
   B. no   D. none of the above

QUESTIONS • COMMENTS • THINGS TO DO

Answers: 1-B; 2-C; 3-B; 4-A; 5-B

PHONE TEN AGENCIES

Phone ten agencies and learn everything you can about their requirements. First ask if they will mail you a copy of their employment requirements and information about upcoming employment examinations. If they will not, ask what their employment requirements are regarding their application process, age, written examination, oral board, physical fitness test, polygraph, current openings, and upcoming openings. Record the information in the space provided below.

Agency	Application Process	Age	Physical Fitness Test	Current Openings	Written Exam	Oral Board	Notes/Other

"Opportunities are usually disguised as hard work, so most people don't recognize them."

—Ann Landers

ACING DATA RECALL QUESTIONS

DATE:

OBJECTIVE:

To improve your data recall abilities.

PURPOSE:

Quick and accurate recall is essential for all police officers. Your written exam will contain recall questions, and by studying today's assignment you will learn some techniques for enhancing your data recall skills. Your improved memory skills will give you a major edge on the written exam. In addition, you will find these memory techniques immensely helpful as you study for your written exam.

TIME REQUIRED: Three hours.

ASSIGNMENTS:

1. Study the section titled "Data Recall."
2. Study the section titled "Recalling Written Material."

DATA RECALL

Remembering a piece of information is a four-stage process. In the first stage, information is perceived, encoded, and stored. This phase is crucial to the rest of the process; how you perceive data has a strong effect on how the data is stored in your mind. In the second stage, short-term memory, information has been processed and stored, but is apt to be forgotten quickly unless it moves on to stage three, long-term memory. When we want to remember a piece of information for a long period of time, even indefinitely, the information is processed into long-term memory. (Long-term memory is usually what a person is referring to when he or she speaks of memory.) The fourth and final phase of remembering is retrieval, the process of recalling a piece of information from mental storage.

Methods to improve memory used to be held in very low regard. They were generally thought to have significance only as night-club gimmicks and were not considered worthy of serious examination. Nobody's laughing now, though, because time and time again these techniques have proven to be extremely effective. Although anyone can easily learn these simple techniques, most people won't bother. The short time you spend learning to enhance your memory skills will yield great results when the time comes for you to take your written exam.

The first step, encoding information, will be most important, as obviously you will not have time to store the immediate test data in long-term memory. The tips and techniques discussed in this section will help you encode information in strong, effective ways, giving you a tremendous edge during your written exam. However, you will also need to learn strong long-term memory techniques to help you study for your police exam. You will find that information in this section as well.

Techniques for improving your memory are based on teaching you to organize the things you learn more effectively and group information in easily handled mental packages. Meaningfulness (association) and amount of interference are factors that influence your ability to encode and retrieve information.

Meaningfulness

The more meaningful a piece of information is to you, the easier it will be for you to remember it. The best way to make new information meaningful is to associate it with things you already know.

Any random piece of information can be made meaningful to you if you associate it with items already stored in your memory, such as strong emotional experiences or familiar images. Any of your five senses can be effectively used to form associations. It's perfectly acceptable for a phrase to remind you of a smell, if that's what helps you remember the information.

Don't stop at one sense when forming associations, if you can possibly find another connection. The more thoroughly you link a new piece of information to previously existing memory data, the easier you will find it to recall that piece of information.

Another extremely effective method of remembering any information is through "story" word association. This method works particularly well if you need to memorize lists. Any number of seemingly unimportant and unrelated items can be memorized by creating a story using all the items. The crazier the story, the easier the information will be to remember.

Here's an example of how this technique works. Let's say you're going to the grocery store to buy eight items, but you don't have a pencil and paper to write them down. Try to remember everything you need: coffee, milk, dog food, eggs, cereal, hamburger, soda, and apples. Pause here for 60 seconds and try to list all eight items without looking at the list. Could you do it? Most people have trouble remembering even a simple list of meaningless information. Even if you did remember all eight items, you probably found it difficult. But by using the word association techniques, you can make it effortless! Here's how.

Make up a little story involving the eight items. Pretend you've just walked into a room; the first thing you see is a steaming hot cup of coffee sitting right in the middle of the floor. You pick it up and start to drink it, but realizing it has no milk in it, you walk over to the refrigerator and open the door, looking for milk. Luckily for you, the entire refrigerator is filled with nothing but carton after carton of milk! Choosing one carton at random, you open it and start to pour the milk into the coffee . . . but to your surprise, nothing but dog food comes out of the milk carton. This is obviously revolting, so you set the cup of coffee down . . . and it tips and falls over, spilling coffee everywhere. You've set it right on top of an egg! It's a plastic egg that was a prize out of the cereal box that you see sitting nearby. The cereal is called "Hamburger Heaven," and all the individual pieces of cereal are shaped like tiny hamburgers. You read the back of the box, which tells you that by sending in two proofs of purchase you can get a free bottle of apple soda.

The beauty of this strategy is that you only have to recall one story instead of trying to remember eight separate items. Now pause again for 60 seconds and try to list the eight items you need at the store, using the story. If you're like most people, you'll remember all eight easily—in fact, you'll find it would be difficult to forget an item. This strategy can be used for the rest of your life in all kinds of situations.

Another effective way to use word association is to picture the things you want to remember, then mentally walk through your house or another familiar place, placing the items to be remembered in corners, on chairs, and so on. To recall the objects, mentally walk through your house again, looking in corners and on chairs to find the images you placed there. This system is very popular with orators, who often use this technique to help them remember all the points, in order, that they want to make in a speech.

Interference

When your associations for two different pieces of information are similar, you may find you have difficulty remembering either piece of data. This effect is known as interference. It is important that you eliminate interference as much as possible. There are several effective and simple techniques for this.

1. **Overlearn information.** Keep rehearsing it even after you think you know it well. The effect of this is to make memories so strong that you simply can't get confused about them. For example, most people when learning to drive a car are confused about using the turn signals. They turn on the left blinker when they mean to use the right, or vice versa, because the two actions required—pushing a lever either up or down—are so similar that there is memory interference. However, after a few months of driving, the correct actions become so automatic that it would be impossible to get it wrong, no matter how similar the actions. Rehearsal has eliminated the interference.

2. **Avoid studying similar material together,** to minimize interference from the beginning. For example, instead of studying history right after political science, separate the topics with something dissimilar, such as chemistry.

3. **Space your learning over time instead of trying to take in large quantities of information at once.** If you overcrowd your brain's processing circuits by trying to absorb too much information in one sitting, you'll have a hard time remembering anything! That's why it is so much more effective to study for a short period every day rather than for a longer period once a week.

4. **Organize material by rhyming it.** "Thirty days hath September, April, June, and November" and "I before E except after C" are good examples. Can you remember how many days hath March with-

out going through the rhyme? Probably not. Rhymes work because they impose external organization on memory; if you remember incorrectly, it doesn't rhyme. And a rhyme is sufficiently dissimilar to other pieces of information in your memory that there is very little interference.

USING THE STORY TECHNIQUE

Make up a story to help you memorize the following list of words, and write it down below.

Ball	Ice cream
Car	Stars
Hat	Staple
Boat	Tissue
Raincoat	Cat

_____

_____

_____

_____

_____

_____

_____

_____

_____

_____

_____

RECALLING WRITTEN MATERIAL

On the written portion of your police exam, you will be asked to read stories about police-related incidents, then answer questions about the stories. You will be given 10 to 20 minutes to read and remember the story without taking notes. The test booklet will then be taken away from you while you answer the questions.

The stories you will be reading are straightforward and the questions you will be asked are not difficult. The trick is learning to remember all the information necessary in the short time you are given. The following tips will help you improve your memory for written material.

1. **Become part of the story.** As you read, mentally project yourself into the scene being described. Pretend you are a bystander or a participant in the action and picture everything the reading describes. The more vividly you can imagine the scene, the more likely it is that you will be able to remember all the relevant details.

This kind of mental projection takes intense concentration. Clear your mind of everything except the story and don't allow yourself to be distracted.

When you create your mental picture, try to insert as many familiar objects, faces, and places into the picture as possible. If the story takes place at a busy intersection, picture an intersection near your house with which you are familiar. This will make the story more real to you and therefore more memorable.

2. **Don't try to memorize the text.** In the short time you've been given to read the story, this will be virtually impossible. Instead, focus on identifying and remembering key facts. Types of key information to look for are discussed later in this section.

3. **Use the memory association techniques discussed earlier in this assignment to help you remember key facts.** For instance, you could follow the grocery list example from earlier in this text and make up a similar story to memorize all the objects found at the scene of the crime. Or the description of the victim may remind you of someone you know; when you picture the scene in your head, use that person's face to portray your victim.

Put all your senses into your imagined scene to build association. If the scene described includes a fire, smell the smoke when you create your mental image. Hear the wailing sirens if second and third officers show up at the scene of the crime.

4. **Ask yourself questions as you read the story.** The process of asking and answering questions in your head will help you remember details that might otherwise slip by unnoticed. If the license plate number of a car is mentioned, mentally ask yourself "What is the license plate number of the car?" and answer the question. The repetition will help you encode the information more effectively and will make it easier for you to remember the number when the time comes to answer the question. This will also help you to anticipate what questions will be asked about the story. By doing this, you will begin to view the scene

with an examiner's eye. This will make it easier for you to decide which details are important and which ones are not.

5. **Don't let your concentration slip** between the time your booklet is collected and the time you are allowed to begin answering questions about the story. It is easy to forget everything you've taken such pains to remember if you begin joking with the person sitting next to you or start thinking about what you're going to eat for dinner. Continue to play through the scene in your mind. This will strengthen your mental grip on the information.

6. **Jot down everything you remember about the story as soon as you are allowed to do so.** Even before you try to answer any questions about the story, write down all the details you can. Your notes don't have to be elaborate, just enough information to help you remember the basic facts. If a bloody knife was found at the scene of the crime, scribbling the word "knife" should be sufficient to remind you of this fact. Immediately writing down information such as time and date of occurrence ensures that you won't forget the information when you turn your attention to other details. In particular, any information that contains numbers or names is easy to confuse or forget. Write it down. Then, and only then, are you ready to begin answering the questions about the story.

Focusing on the Key Facts

The easiest and most reliable way to identify the key facts in a story is to focus on the six items that must be contained in any thorough report of a police incident: when, where, who, what, how, and why. The word NEOTWY, derived by taking the last letter from each of the six key items, is a good memory aid.

```
wheN
wherE
whO
whaT
hoW
whY
```

Because these six items sum up the information crucial to any good police report, if you simply remember each piece of information, you should be able to answer any questions based on the story you have read. To make it even easier, there are common types of information that are found in each of the six categories.

When? Always remember any times and/or dates given in the story; it is likely you will be asked for this information. Common information given includes time of occurrence, time of reporting, and time of arrest. Don't forget to include the date with the time; "10:00 A.M., Friday, May 12."

Where? You will need to know where incidents happen and where evidence is located, if this information is given in the story. If compass directions are mentioned (north, south, east, west), make sure you remember them. They will be important. If more than one incident occurs in the story, remember where each one took place.

Who? Witnesses, victims, perpetrators, and accomplices are standard fixtures in every police report. Remember the descriptions and characteristics of each one. If the report states that the perpetrator was six feet tall with a scar on his forehead and the accomplice was five and a half feet tall, remember who is who! You will probably be asked to remember the identifying characteristics and to differentiate between the two.

What? This item basically covers the overall scene. What happened? What crime was committed? What did the police do? What did the site of the incident look like? Your mental picture should answer most of these details if you've created a strong image.

How? Ask yourself two questions to answer this category: "How many?" and "How did it happen?" How many perpetrators? How many officers responded? How was the crime committed? Whether a weapon was used, along with the weapon's description, is an essential part of this category.

Why? Motive is the primary piece of information covered by this category. Make sure you know why the incident occurred. If several possible motives are given, remember all of them. If there isn't substantial evidence to indicate the motive, simply say, "Motive unknown as at this time." Don't guess.

Checklist of Data Recall Techniques

Meaningfulness
- ✓ Associate random pieces of information with items already in your memory.
- ✓ Don't use only one sense to form associations.
- ✓ Make up a story using the items to be memorized.
- ✓ Take a mental walk through your house, placing items to be memorized where you can see them.

Interference
- ✓ Overlearn information.
- ✓ Avoid studying similar material together.

- ✓ Space your learning over time.
- ✓ Organize material by rhyming it.

Written Material
- ✓ Become part of the story.
- ✓ Don't try to memorize the text; focus on key facts.
- ✓ Use memory association techniques to remember key facts.
- ✓ Put all your senses into your images.
- ✓ Ask yourself questions as you read the story.
- ✓ Don't let your concentration slip after your booklet is collected.
- ✓ Jot down everything you remember about the story as soon as possible.

QUESTIONS • COMMENTS • THINGS TO DO

STEP

9

"Success often comes to those who dare to act; it seldom goes to the timid, who are ever afraid of the consequences."

—**Jawa Harlal Nehru**

Visual Detection and Observation and Phone Ten Agencies

DATE:

OBJECTIVE:

To understand and practice visual detection and observation techniques and to phone ten agencies.

PURPOSE:

The ability to recognize objects or faces that have been made to look different is a skill you will use constantly throughout your law enforcement career, as is the ability to take in and remember large quantities of visual information quickly and accurately. You will be tested on these abilities. This section will help you master these skills in preparation for your police exam and for your law enforcement career.

By phoning ten agencies, you will continue to gather information necessary for your application process.

TIME REQUIRED: Two hours.

ASSIGNMENTS:

1. Study the section titled "Visual Detection and Observation" and answer sample questions.
2. Phone ten agencies.

VISUAL DETECTION AND OBSERVATION

An important responsibility of a law enforcement officer is being able to recognize objects and faces that have been made to look different. A stolen bicycle might be painted a different color, or a criminal you're after may have grown a beard since the last time you saw him. You must be able to see through the changes and identify the object or person you're after.

Consider the case of a trial where a witness cries out, "Yes, that's him! I saw him do it!" Even if the testimony is later discredited due to poor lighting at the scene of the crime or the witness's poor eyesight, the jury is much more likely to convict the defendant than it would be without a positive identification. Humans are sight-oriented creatures; being able to say with assurance that you recognize something—and be right about it—will make a big impression every time. And not only will you need to be able to answer visual detection questions on your police exam, this skill will be invaluable to you in your law enforcement career.

Visual detection is not necessarily a natural ability. It's a skill and, like any skill, it can be learned and developed. The key to visual detection is recall, the active reconstruction of information. It involves searching for and finding pieces of information. It also involves a person's knowledge, attitudes, and expectations. Therefore the more you are able to relate something you are looking at to your personal experience, the better your visual recall will be.

The easiest way to do this is to focus on the details. As you look at objects on your exam, try to associate them with something you've seen before, or even something you have around your house. Perhaps the object will trigger a memory about something that happened to you in the past. By creating a mental link between the object and that event, you've made it very unlikely that you will forget what the test object looks like.

If it's a face you're looking at, does it look like someone you know? Perhaps the shape of the head, eyes, ears, nose, or mouth can be associated with someone else. You can also associate features with objects. Maybe the person's head is perfectly round, reminding you of a basketball. Once you form that association, you're not likely to confuse that person with someone who has an oval head.

Use all your senses in forming these mental links. If the object or person pictured on the test doesn't remind you of anything visually, start going through the other categories—smell, sound, feel, taste. One of them is bound to strike a chord. Needless to say, the more senses you can involve in your mental link, the better. Don't stop at one unless you just can't seem to find another association, or you are running out of time.

By becoming proficient at these visual detection techniques, you will ensure that you are fully prepared for your police exam.

Use these techniques along with the ones for studying pictures that follow to answer the sample questions at the end of this section.

STUDYING PICTURES

Police exams often test applicants on their memory of pictures and wanted posters. Being able to study a picture and then answer detailed questions about it once it has been removed from sight is a skill you need to develop in order to be successful on the written exam. Use the following techniques to prepare for this portion of the exam.

1. **Study the picture in an organized way.** You cannot simply stare at a picture for several minutes and then expect to remember the relevant information; your mind is not recording the information unless you are making a conscious effort to remember each detail. Be methodical! Proceed from one section of the picture to another, making mental notes of each object. Silently describe to yourself what you are seeing. Forming the words in your head will give shape to your observations and will make details easier to remember.

2. **The important details to remember are when, where, who, what, how and why—NEOTWY.** NEOTWY is a memory device that comes from taking the last letter of each of the six important categories of information:

wheN
wherE
whO
whaT
hoW
whY

Start your observation of the picture by answering these six questions.

When: Remember anything in the picture that gives you a hint of the time. Is it day or night? Are any clocks or calendars pictured?

Where: Is the picture inside or outside? Is there any indication of the geographic location of the picture, such as a street sign or address? Notice the location of individual items in the picture. Where are things in relation to each other? Is the woman to the right or the left of the man? Where is the gun?

Who: Take particular notice of any people in the picture. What are they wearing? What do they look like? Do they have any distinguishing characteristics? Is there anything unusual about any of the people? Also take particular notice of items near each person. This is important because, in questions, people are usually identified by what they are near in the picture. The examiner may ask, "What is the sex of the person standing next to the car?" If you've already identified the people in your own mind by their relation to the objects around them, you'll have no problem with these questions.

What: What is happening in the picture (what is the overall scene)? Take note of the details of what is going on; tell the story to yourself in your mind to help you remember each detail. Also, what is happening in other parts of the picture? The overall scene may involve a police incident, but a smaller scene may be taking place in another part of the picture. Perhaps two people are shown having dinner together in a nearby restaurant, taking no notice of the incident going on.

How: How did the pictured scene come about? If a crime was committed, how was it accomplished?

Why: Continually ask yourself why a certain thing is happening. Why is the lady crying? Why is the car on the right instead of the left side of the street? Take particular notice of anything unusual in the picture.

3. **Look for "readable's" in the picture.** You will almost certainly be asked about them. Are there any clocks, signs, license plates, T-shirt slogans or any other readable text? If there is, read it carefully and remember it.

4. **Keep an eye open for unusual things.** Is a window broken? Are any weapons visible? Is anything out of place in the picture or placed in an unusual position?

5. **Count all objects.** Always make a quick count of major objects, including cars, bystanders, police officers, animals, bicycles, etc.

6. Use the memory association techniques discussed in Step 8, "Acing Data Recall Questions," to help you remember key facts. For instance, you could follow the grocery list example and make up a story to memorize all the objects you notice in the picture. **Don't rely exclusively on rote memory!**

7. **Don't stop examining the picture when you've completed all the above steps.** If you run through the list of things to examine before your time runs out, do it again, and again, and again. The more times you can go through the checklist, the stronger your memory will be.

8. Don't let your concentration slip between the time your booklet is collected and the time you are allowed to begin answering questions about the story. It is easy to forget everything you've taken such pains to remember if you begin joking with the person sitting next to you or start thinking about what you're going to eat for dinner. **Continue to examine the picture in your mind.** This will strengthen your mental grip on the information.

9. **Jot down everything you remember about the picture as soon as you are allowed to do so.** Do this before you even try to answer any questions. Your notes don't have to be elaborate; write down just enough information to help you remember the basic facts. If a car appears in the bottom left corner of the picture, scribbling the words "car, bot. L" or something similar should be sufficient to remind you of this fact. In particular, any information that contains words or numbers, such as license plate numbers or street names, is easy to confuse or forget. Write it down. Then, and only then, are you ready to begin answering the questions about the picture.

OBSERVATION

For questions 1 to 10, choose the correct answer based on the following picture. You may not refer back to the scene.

OBSERVATION QUESTIONS

1. How many men are in the picture?
   A. four
   B. five
   C. six
   D. none of the above

2. How many uniformed officers are in the picture?

   A. four   C. six

   B. five   D. none of the above

3. How many men are walking?

   A. one   C. three

   B. two   D. none of the above

4. How many windows does the largest building have?

   A. ten   C. seventeen

   B. twelve   D. none of the above

5. The doors to the big building are

   A. open   C. closed

   B. partially open   D. none of the above

6. Does the sidewalk continue across the roadway?

   A. yes   B. no

7. Is the cat in the picture facing the buildings?

   A. yes   B. no

8. Where is the guardhouse in relation to the gate as you look at the picture?

   A. left   B. right

9. What is the guard closest to the main building doing?

   A. smiling   C. sitting

   B. writing   D. waving

10. How many men in the picture are carrying briefcases?

    A. none   C. two

    B. one   D. three

VISUAL DETECTION

For questions 1 to 5, choose the correct answer based on the following sets of drawings.

1. Which outline matches the picture in the box?

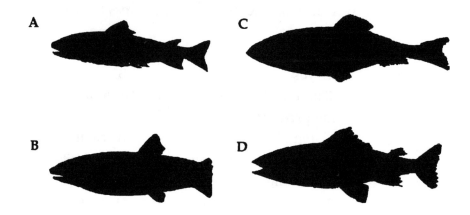

2. Which outline matches the picture in the box?

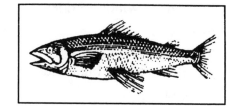

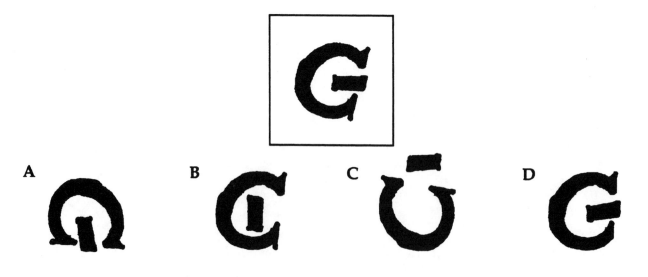

3. Which outline matches the picture in the box?

 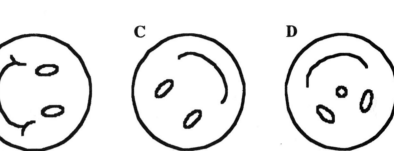

4. Which outline matches the picture in the box?

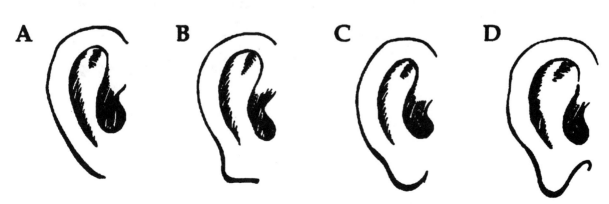

5. Which outline matches the picture in the box?

VISUAL DETECTION—WANTED POSTERS

For questions 1 to 6, choose the correct answer. You may not refer back to the poster.

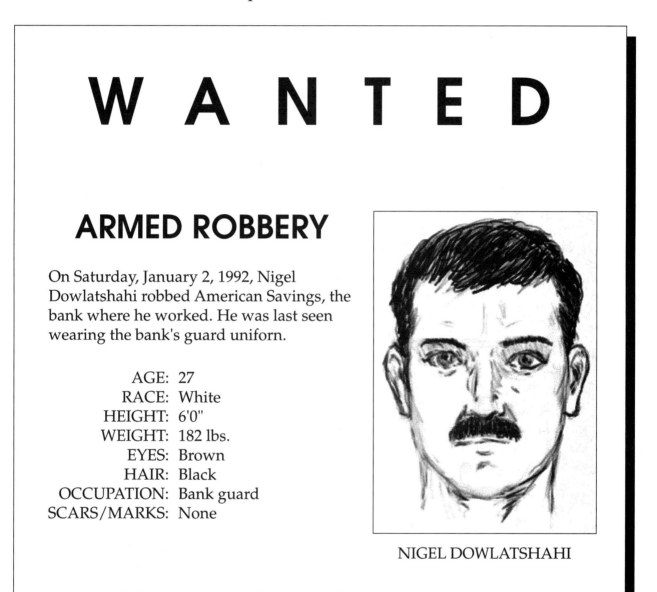

WANTED

ARMED ROBBERY

On Saturday, January 2, 1992, Nigel Dowlatshahi robbed American Savings, the bank where he worked. He was last seen wearing the bank's guard uniforn.

AGE:	27
RACE:	White
HEIGHT:	6'0"
WEIGHT:	182 lbs.
EYES:	Brown
HAIR:	Black
OCCUPATION:	Bank guard
SCARS/MARKS:	None

NIGEL DOWLATSHAHI

Subjects entered in the National Crime Information Center
CAUTION: ARMED AND DANGEROUS

1. This man's name is
   A. Nigel Dowlatshahi   C. Dowlat Nigel
   B. Nigel Dollatshah   D. none of the above

2. This man's height is
   A. 5'10"   C. 6'2'
   B. 6'0"   D. none of the above

3. This man is wanted for
   A. armed robbery   C. murder
   B. burglary   D. none of the above

4. This man weighs
   A. 172 lbs.   C. 192 lbs.
   B. 182 lbs.   D. none of the above

5. This man's age is
   A. 27   C. 38
   B. 39   D. none of the above

6. Is this person armed and dangerous?
   A. yes   B. no

PHONE TEN AGENCIES

Phone ten agencies and learn everything you can about their requirements. First ask if they will mail you a copy of their employment requirements and information about upcoming employment examinations. If they will not, ask what their employment requirements are regarding their application process, age, written examination, oral board, physical fitness test, polygraph, current openings, and upcoming openings. Record the information in the space provided below.

Agency	Application Process	Age	Physical Fitness Test	Current Openings	Written Exam	Oral Board	Notes/Other

"Success is failure turned inside out, The silver tint of the clouds of doubt, And you can never tell how close you are. It may be near when it seems so far. So stick to the fight when you're hardest hit, It's when things seem worse that you must not quit."

—Unknown

IMPORTANT LEGAL TERMS

DATE:

OBJECTIVE:

To become familiar with legal terms that are often used in the course of police work.

PURPOSE:

A thorough knowledge of legal terms will be essential in your law enforcement career. Some of the terms discussed in today's assignment do not have precise legal definitions, but are frequently used in legal and police contexts. Many police exams have sections that test your knowledge of common legal terms. You will need to have a basic legal vocabulary to answer these questions correctly.

In addition, you will find it helpful during your oral interview to be able to refer to procedures and situations using their correct legal terms. It's not required that you do so, but it will be noticed by your interviewers. Remember, any edge helps!

Today's assignment is not intended to give you a complete knowledge of all legal terms and their implications. It is merely designed to give you a basic familiarity with their usage.

TIME REQUIRED: Four hours.

ASSIGNMENT:

1. Learn the legal terms contained in this section.
2. Complete the "Legal Terms Checklist" as you master each definition.

LEGAL TERMS CHECKLIST

Check off each word as you feel confident that you know its definition. Continue to review the legal definitions that follow until you are comfortable with the entire list of terms.

___ Acquittal

___ Affirm

___ Affirmative action

___ Arraignment

___ Arrest

___ Bench trial

___ Bind-over hearing

___ Career criminals

___ Challenge for cause

___ Change of venue

___ Charging the jury

___ Citation

___ Clearance rate

___ Common law crime

___ Concurrent sentence

___ Conjugal visits

___ Consecutive sentence

___ Consolidation of police services

___ Contracting of police department services

___ Conviction

___ Corrections

___ Crime

___ Criminal statutes

___ Criterion-related entrance tests

___ Decriminalization

___ Deterrence

___ Disclosure of presentence report

___ Discovery

___ Dismissal

___ Double jeopardy

___ Due process

___ Entrapment

___ Felony

___ Flat sentence

___ Frisk

___ Good faith defense

___ Goodtime credit laws

___ Grand jury

___ Impeachment

___ Indeterminate sentence

___ Index crimes

___ Indictment

___ Indigent defendant

___ Initial court appearance

___ Involuntary confession

___ Judgment

___ Jurisdiction

___ Jury nullification

___ Lateral entry

___ LEAA

___ LEEP

___ Mens rea

___ Misdemeanor

___ No bill

___ Nolo contendere

___ Omnibus Crime Control and Safe Streets Act of 1968

___ Overcriminalization

___ Parens patriae

___ Peremptory challenge

___ Preliminary hearing

___ Presentence report

___ Presumptive sentence

___ Preventive detention

___ Probable cause

___ Punitive damages

___ Reactive patrol

___ Recidivism

___ Retribution

___ Reversal

___ Reverse and remand

___ Stop and frisk

___ Summons

___ Team policing

___ Transcript

___ Trial de novo

___ Uniform Crime Reports

___ Venire

___ Verdict

___ Victim compensation

___ Voir dire

___ Waiver

___ Warrant

___ Writ of certiorari

___ Writ of habeas corpus

IMPORTANT LEGAL TERMS

Acquittal A decision that the defendant is not guilty of the charges against him or her beyond a reasonable doubt.

Affirm The decision made by appeals court to let stand the conviction or sentence from a trial court.

Affirmative action Special programs and efforts to recruit and hire minority group members and to eliminate the sources and effects of past and present employment discrimination.

Arraignment Stage at which the defendant is brought before a trial court, hears the charges read, and is asked to enter a plea to each charge.

Arrest Being taken into custody prior to being formally charged with a crime.

Bench trial Legal proceeding in which a decision is made regarding the defendant's guilt or innocence, made by the court alone. The decision is expressed in a judgment. See also judgment.

Bind-over hearing Hearing where probable cause is established and the case is bound over for grand jury action. See also preliminary hearing.

Career criminals Recidivist, professional criminals and other offenders who choose to lead lives of crime and who are successful at avoiding punishment.

Challenge for cause The attempt by the prosecutor or defense counsel to remove a prospective juror during voir dire on the grounds that the juror is unfit to serve or would not be impartial.

Change of venue Holding a trial other than where a crime was committed in order to ensure a fair trial for the defendant.

Charging the jury Verbal instructions given to the jury describing law principles that should guide the jury's deliberations and verdict.

Citation Written notice ordering a person to appear in court. Usually used for petty offenses.

Clearance rate The percentage of crimes reported to police that are said to be solved.

Common law crime Identification of crimes by early English courts before legislatures were fully operational.

Concurrent sentence Prison sentence in which separate terms are served at the same time. Thus the actual sentence is the longest single term imposed, not the sum of all terms.

Conjugal visits Programs that allow the prisoner's spouse, children, and other family members to spend time with the prisoner in private quarters.

Consecutive sentence Prison sentence in which separate terms are added together to arrive at the total time to be served.

Consolidation of police services An agreement between two or more jurisdictions to perform certain services jointly.

Contracting of police department services An arrangement whereby a police department purchases services from the private sector or larger police departments.

Conviction Decision that the defendant is guilty beyond a reasonable doubt.

Corrections Term encompassing probation, institutions, and parole.

Crime Violation of criminal statutes (penal code) or the acts of Congress.

Criminal statutes The body of law that defines crimes and their penalties.

Criterion-related entrance tests   Tests that are related to objective measures of performance, designed to carry no cultural bias.

Decriminalization   The moderation of victimless crimes, especially substituting fines for incarceration.

Deterrence   The threat or imposition of punishment.

Disclosure of presentence report   Making the contents of the presentence report available to the defendant and defense counsel.

Discovery   The process by which prosecutor and defense counsel study each other's cases and set up strategies for obtaining a conviction or an acquittal.

Dismissal   Termination of prosecution due to lack of evidence.

Double jeopardy   Provision of the Fifth Amendment that prevents individuals from being tried twice for the same crime.

Due process   Procedures that are followed to ensure citizens receive fair and proper treatment under the criminal justice system. Based on the Fourteenth Amendment, which says no state shall "deprive any person of life, liberty, or property, without due process of law."

Entrapment   Said to exist when a person who did not intend to commit a crime did so due to police enticement.

Felony   A crime punishable by death or incarceration, usually for one year or more.

Flat sentence   A sentence in which a defendant is sentenced to a specific number of years in prison.

Frisk   Pat-down of a person's outer clothing to discover potential weapons.

Good faith defense   Used in a suit against the police. Its premise is that even though the officer lacked probable cause according to the law, her, he, or she nonetheless acted in a reasonable manner given the circumstances.

Goodtime credit laws   Laws that reduce prison time that must be served before being eligible for parole by deducting from the sentence time for the following: a. each month or year spent in prison; b. participating in prison industry; and c. being a model prisoner.

Grand jury   A group of sixteen to twenty-three citizens responsible for deciding whether there is probable cause to indict a defendant on the criminal charges presented by the prosecutor.

Impeachment   An indictment by the United States House of Representatives. It is the first step in removing corrupt federal officials.

Indeterminate sentence   Sentence that provides a range of time to be served, such as 2 to 5 years or 10 to 20 years.

Index crimes   There are seven index offenses: willful homicide, forcible rape, robbery, aggravated assault, burglary, larceny-theft, and motor vehicle theft. Selected for their seriousness, frequency and likelihood of being reported, they serve as an index of the amount, trends, and changes in crime nationwide.

Indictment   1. A written accusation charging the defendant with specific crimes. 2. Grand jury decision that there is probable cause to arraign the defendant on charges in the written accusation.

Indigent defendant   A defendant who is too poor to hire a lawyer. He or she is given free defense counsel in the form of court–assigned counsel or a public defender.

Initial court appearance   Also called the presentment, first arraignment, or preliminary arraignment , it is the first processing stage after arrest, in which the defendant is taken before a magistrate. Its purposes are to inform defendants of their constitutional rights, to supply indigent defendants with free defense counsel, and to set bail.

Involuntary confession A confession made without the suspect's having been read the Miranda rights or having waived such rights.

Judgment The decision made by a judge regarding the defendant's guilt or innocence.

Jurisdiction The court's authority to preside over, handle, and decide the issues in specific kinds of cases.

Jury nullification Refusal or reluctance of the jury to convict in capital cases because of the severity of the sentence involved.

Lateral entry The opportunity to join police departments at an advanced rank and to be given credit for prior service, experience, and achievement when applying for positions in other agencies.

LEAA The Law Enforcement Assistance Administration, a federal agency created by the Safe Streets Act of 1968 to distribute crime control funds to state and local governments.

LEEP The Law Enforcement Education Program, a component of the LEAA that subsidizes the higher education of preservice criminal justice students and inservice criminal justice practitioners.

Mens rea "Guilty mind" or criminal intent; state of mind at the time the crime was committed. Criminal intent must be established before the offender can be held responsible for criminal behavior.

Misdemeanor A crime punishable by a fine or imprisonment, usually for no more than one year.

No bill The refusal of the grand jury to indict. Results in dismissal of the case.

Nolo contendere A plea of "no contest" to charges. The defendant indirectly admits guilt by not claiming innocence, but avoids having a formal admission of guilt on record.

Omnibus Crime Control and Safe Streets Act of 1968 Federal legislation passed in the 1960s to assist state and local governments in improving their criminal justice systems. See also LEAA.

Overcriminalization The belief that too many activities are regulated and that victimless crimes should be decriminalized and ultimately legalized.

Parens patriae Theory that views the juvenile court as taking the role of parent to assure the custody and retrying the case as new.

Peremptory challenge A request for removal of a prospective juror during voir dire without a reason being given.

Preliminary hearing (see *also bind-over hearing*) A hearing requiring the state to establish probable cause that the defendant committed a crime. Protects a defendant against unwarranted prosecution and detention.

Presentence report A report prepared by the probation officer that contains a nonbinding recommendation for disposition of a convicted defendant. Used as a sentencing aid for the court.

Presumptive sentence System of standard flat prison terms based on the relative seriousness of the crime committed. Subject to slight variation.

Preventive detention The imprisonment of defendants awaiting trial who are believed to be capable of committing serious new crimes if released on bail while awaiting trial. Achieved by setting high bail that the defendant cannot raise.

Probable cause   Reasonable grounds to believe that the person arrested is the felon who committed a certain crime. Also the legal basis on which warrants are issued and on which defendants are bound over from the preliminary hearing to the grand jury.

Punitive damages   Damages levied by a civil court of jury against the defendant as a punishment for wrongful actions.

Reactive patrol   A patrol strategy in which the police respond to information from outside the department, i.e. citizen calls for assistance.

Recidivist   A person who constantly commits crimes and seems unable to be cured of criminal tendencies; a persistent or repeat offender.

Retribution   The belief that the punishment should fit the crime.

Reversal   Decision of the appeals court to overturn the conviction or sentence obtained in trial court.

Reverse and remand   Situation in which the appeals court overturns the decision of a trial court and returns the case to the trial court judge with instructions on how to rectify the errors of law.

Stop and frisk   Practice of stopping persons exhibiting suspicious behavior, questioning them for identification purposes and patting down the outer clothing of those whose answers or conduct either arouse further suspicion or threaten the officer involved.

Summons   A written notice ordering a person to appear in court. Usually used for specific petty offenses.

Team policing   A team of officers functioning as generalist-specialists. Officers are given fixed, continuous and expanded responsibilities within a certain geographical area.

Transcript   A written record of judicial or administrative proceedings. The transcript is very important in appealing convictions or sentences.

Trial de novo   The setting aside of the decision of a court with limited jurisdiction and retrying the case as new.

Uniform Crime Reports   A national annual compilation of crime statistics based on information provided by local police departments to the FBI.

Venire   The initial list of potential jurors from which the final list of actual jurors is selected.

Verdict   The decision of guilt or innocence made by a petit jury at the conclusion of a trial.

Victim compensation   State payments made to victims of violent crime for medical bills and income lost due to injuries received.

Voir dire   The questioning of prospective jurors to determine their fitness to serve in the trial in question and to eliminate jurors who would not be impartial.

Waiver   The decision of a defendant or convicted offender to relinquish a legal right.

Warrant   A court order directing the police to arrest a certain person or authorizing them to search a particular place and/or area.

Writ of certiorari   A petition requesting the Supreme Court to review the legality of a conviction or a sentence.

Writ of habeas corpus   Used by the defense counsel to have the accused brought before court to determine whether the defendant's detention and confinement are legal.

"There is no future in any job. The future lies in the man who holds the job."

—**George Crane**

BASIC MATH SKILLS

DATE:

OBJECTIVE:

To review basic math skills.

PURPOSE:

Although not all law enforcement employment exams include mathematics sections, it is important to be prepared. By reviewing the basic math skills contained in this section, you will ensure success on this portion of the written exam.

TIME REQUIRED: Three hours.

ASSIGNMENT:

1. Review the math skills and examples contained in the section titled "Review of Basic Math Skills." Review the material for as long as necessary to give you a solid grasp of the subject.
2. Answer the sample questions.

REVIEW OF BASIC MATH SKILLS

Multiplication by Tens

When multiplying a number by 10 or by a multiple of 10, such as 100 or 1,000, move the decimal point to the right the number of spaces equal to the number of zeros in the multiplier. For instance, $4.3 \times 10 = 43.0$ or just 43. There is one zero in 10, so the decimal point was moved one space to the right, putting it after the 3. Likewise, $0.75 \times 100 = 75.0$ or 75; the decimal point moved two places because there are two zeros in 100.

For whole numbers (those that do not have any decimal points), remember that there is an invisible decimal point that is understood to appear just to the right of the final digit in the number. Thus, 67 is the same as 67.; 132 is the same as 132.; etc.

> **Examples:** $0.074 \times 100 = 7.4$
> $0.85 \times 100 = 85$
> $8.3 \times 10 = 83$
> $21 \times 100 = 2,100$
> $34 \times 1,000 = 34,000$

Division by Tens

Dividing by tens is just as easy. Use the same rules that apply to multiplication by tens, but change the direction you move the decimal point. When dividing, move the decimal point to the left instead of to the right. Remember where the decimal point is assumed to be if it does not appear in the number—to the right of the final digit.

> **Examples:** $0.1326 \div 100 = .001326$
> $0.81 \div 100 = .0081$
> $2.6 \div 10 = .26$
> $31 \div 100 = .31$
> $44 \div 1,000 = .044$

Adding and Subtracting Decimals

When adding or subtracting numbers with decimals, be sure to keep the decimals in line. Once you've lined up all the numbers, add and subtract as you would normally, ignoring the decimal point. Just make sure you include the decimal—in the same place as it falls in the column above—in your answer.

You will probably find it easiest to insert zeros where necessary to maintain the alignment of the columns.

Example:	.106 + 31 + 281.14 + .0084 + 6.14 + 13		
Becomes:	.106	or	000.1060
	31.		031.0000
	281.14		281.1400
	.0084		000.0084
	6.14		006.1400
	13.		013.0000
			331.3944

Multiplying by Decimals

When multiplying by decimals, ignore the decimal point until you reach the final product. Then place the decimal point so that the number of digits to its right is equal to the sum of the places to the right of the decimal points in the numbers being multiplied.

Example:	2.142	Three digits to the right of the decimal point
	× 0.31	Two digits to the right of the decimal point
	0.66402	3 + 2 = 5 digits to the right of the decimal point

Dividing by Decimals

When dividing by decimals, move the decimal point in both numbers to the right an equal number of spaces until the divisor (the number being divided into the other) becomes a whole number (one without a decimal point). The decimal point in the answer lies directly above the decimal point in the dividend (the number being divided by the other).

Example: $.3\overline{)60}$ becomes $3\overline{)600}$ = 200

Example: $\dfrac{3}{4} + \dfrac{5}{6} + \dfrac{2}{9} + \dfrac{6}{15}$

Factor each denominator into prime numbers

$$\dfrac{=3}{(2 \times 2)} \qquad \dfrac{=5}{(2 \times 3)} \qquad \dfrac{=2}{(3 \times 3)} \qquad \dfrac{=6}{(3 \times 5)}$$

To find the lowest common denominator (LCD), take the highest power of each prime number appearing and multiply them: $(2 \times 2)(3 \times 3)(5)$

$= (4)(9)(5)$

$= 180$

Divide each denominator into the LCD and multiply this quotient by the numerator. Place this number over the LCD.

$$\frac{(180 \div 4) \times 3}{180} + \frac{(180 \div 6) \times 5}{180} + \frac{(180 \div 9) \times 2}{180} + \frac{(180 \div 15) \times 6}{180}$$

$$= \frac{(45 \times 3)}{180} + \frac{(30 \times 5)}{180} + \frac{(20 \times 2)}{180} + \frac{(12 \times 6)}{180}$$

$$= \frac{135}{180} + \frac{150}{180} + \frac{40}{180} + \frac{72}{180}$$

$$= \frac{397}{180} = \frac{237}{180}$$

Example: $\dfrac{8}{12} \times \dfrac{12}{16} \times \dfrac{3}{9} \times \dfrac{5}{15}$

$$= \frac{2}{3} \times \frac{3}{4} \times \frac{1}{3} \times \frac{1}{3}$$

$$= \frac{6}{108} = \frac{1}{18}$$

Example: $\dfrac{1}{4} \div \dfrac{7}{8} = \dfrac{1}{4} \times \dfrac{8}{7} = \dfrac{8}{28} = \dfrac{2}{7}$

$$4 \div \frac{1}{3} = 4 \times 3 = 12$$

$$\frac{3}{5} \div 3 = \frac{3}{5} \times \frac{1}{3} = \frac{3}{15} = \frac{1}{5}$$

Word Problems

Nearly every kind of mathematical concept or problem can be translated into a form of word problem. What they all have in common is the translation of mathematical symbols and ideas into words. Therefore, it's your obligation to translate them back again. Study the list of equivalents that follows. It is not exhaustive, but it does contain the most common words and their mathematical counterparts. Whenever you encounter one of the words or phrases from this list you should automatically think of applying the appropriate mathematical procedure.

Addition	Subtraction	Multiplication	Division
Total	Minus	Times	Average
Sum	Less	Product	To find the time in
Plus	Difference	Twice	work problems
Altogether	Smaller than	Tripled, quadrupled,	To find the rate in
More than	Younger than	etc.	work problems
Length	Years ago	Percent of	Quotient
Gain	Less expensive by	Fraction of	
More expensive by	Decreased by	Squared, cubed, etc.	
Increased by	Diminished by	Area	
Exceeds by	Reduced by	Volume	
Longer by	Cheaper	To find the distance	
Years from now	Lighter	in motion prob-	
Older	Remainder	lems	
	How much more than	To find the work in	
		work problems	

SAMPLE PROBLEMS

1. $24 \times 100 =$
2. $3.71 \times 100 =$
3. $92.3 \div 10 =$
4. $.0179 \times 100 =$
5. $.085 \div 100 =$
6. $1,132 \div 1,000 =$
7. $541 \times 10 =$
8. $8,957.32 \div 100 =$
9. $0.470 \times 1,000 =$
10. $27 \times 10,000 =$
11. Add 1.63 to 0.725.
12. Add 39.82 and 74.04.
13. Subtract 0.66 from 0.87.
14. The difference between 92.842 and 7.382 is?
15. The sum of 38 and 34.34 is?
16. Take 3.53 away from 56.89.
17. What is 734.5 plus 23.323?
18. Add 0.68 and 0.773.
19. What is 0.12 minus 0.003?
20. Subtract 0.599 from 4.004.
21. Multiply 3.65 times 9.3.
22. Divide 8.45 by 0.32.
23. The product of 0.656 and 34.1 is?
24. Thirteen multiplied by 3.75 is?
25. The quotient of 32.5 and 6.78 is?

26. Divide 0.54 into 0.93.
27. The product of 0.6 and 0.088 is?
28. 0.49 into 234 is?
29. 6.04 multiplied by 39.51 is?
30. Find the quotient of 76.98 and 4.4.
31. 1/2 plus 3/4 is?
32. 7/8 minus 1/6 is?
33. 5/12 plus 7/3 is?
34. 1/9 plus 1/3 is?
35. 3/8 minus 2/9 is?
36. 7/6 minus 2/15 is?
37. 1/3 plus 3/5 plus 1/2 is?
38. 12/17 minus 4/8 minus 1/3 is?
39. 7/5 plus 3/4 plus 3/2 is?
40. 14/37 minus 4/9 is?
41. Multiply 3/2 by 6/7.
42. Divide 3/4 by 1/2.
43. 7 divided by 4/5 is?
44. The product of 1/3 and 3/5 is?
45. Divide 5/4 into 3/7.
46. The quotient of 8/9 and 2/5 is?
47. 1/4 into 2/3 is?
48. 7/12 times 9/16 is?
49. The product of 1/2 and 1/3 and 1/4 is?
50. 2/3 divided by 7/8 divided by 5 is?

Answers to Sample Problems

1. 2,400	15. 72.34	29. 238.6404	43. 8 3/4
2. 371	16. 53.36	30. 17.495	44. 1/5
3. 9.23	17. 757.823	31. 1 1/4	45. 12/35
4. 1.79	18. 1.453	32. 17/24	46. 2 2/9
5. .00085	19. 0.117	33. 2 3/4	47. 2 2/3
6. 1.132	20. 3.405	34. 4/9	48. 21/64
7. 5410	21. 33.945	35. 11/72	49. 1/24
8. 89.5732	22. 26.40625	36. 1 1/30	50. 16/105
9. 470	23. 22.3696	37. 1 13/30	
10. 270,000	24. 48.75	38. −13/102	
11. 2.355	25. 4.79	39. 3 13/20	
12. 113.86	26. 1.72	40. −22/333	
13. 0.21	27. .0528	41. 1 2/7	
14. 85.460	28. 477.551	42. 1 1/2	

QUESTIONS • COMMENTS • THINGS TO DO

"Going far beyond the call of duty, doing more than others expect . . . this is what excellence is all about. And it comes from striving, maintaining the highest standards, looking after the smallest detail, and going the extra mile. Excellence means doing your best. In everything. In every way."

—Unknown

INCREASE YOUR READING COMPREHENSION SKILLS

DATE:

OBJECTIVE:

To increase your reading comprehension skills.

PURPOSE:

Reading skill is the foundation upon which all other study skills build. If you have difficulty understanding what you read, you will have difficulty studying and learning. It's as simple as that. For that reason, you must increase your reading skill. There is nothing else you can do that will help you as much in the long run as learning to be an effective reader.

Besides helping you study, your increased reading comprehension skills will help you greatly on your written exam, as you must, of course, read—and understand what you have read—throughout the exam.

TIME REQUIRED: Three hours.

ASSIGNMENTS:

1. Study the section titled "How to Be a Better Reader."
2. Study the section titled "Strategies for Reading Comprehension Tests."

HOW TO BE A BETTER READER

There are two primary ways to read—for reference and critical reading. Knowing when to use each will make any assignment easier.

Reading for Reference

You should read for reference when looking for specific information. In this type of reading, you are searching for clues to solve a specific problem without regard to the overall meaning of the text. For example, if you want to find a piece of information about dogs in a book on animals, you might flip through the pages looking for headings that seemed to relate to dogs. If a heading seemed promising, you would then skim the text under that heading to see if the appropriate fact was there. If not, you would continue to glance through the book until you found the correct heading and the information for which you were searching. You would not read the entire book.

Critical Reading

Also referred to as study reading, critical reading is necessary when the reader needs to understand concepts, ideas, or thoughts—items demanding analysis and concentration. In order to understand the text fully, the reader must relate it to his or her own experiences and come to conclusions about the concepts being presented. The arguments, when added up, must make sense to the reader if the basic premise is to be accepted.

The best way to tackle any reading assignment, whether simple or complicated, is to skim the text first to get an idea of the type of information included. Read any titles, headings, or subheads. In addition, most text is organized so that the key point of any paragraph is made in the first sentence of that paragraph; succeeding sentences add detail to the main idea. Read the key sentence of each paragraph in your first run-through.

Once you have a basic familiarity with the text, go back and start again from the beginning, this time reading with full concentration. Take notes as necessary.

Once you're ready to begin a thorough reading of the text, use the exercise described below to help organize your thoughts and increase your understanding of the information. Read one section at a time. At the end of each section, complete the following exercise:

1. Jot down definitions of any key terms included in the section.
2. Write down any questions and answers you feel clarify the topic.
3. Write down any questions for which you don't know the answers, and then make sure you find them. If the text doesn't make a point sufficiently clear, do further research if necessary.
4. Even if you still have unanswered questions, move on to the next section. You may find the answers later in the text.

Complete the above exercise for each section of your reading. (At the end of Step 12 is a Reading Comprehension Summary chart that you can copy and use as a study aid.)

Note that there are some exceptions to rule four, which tells you to go on even if you do not completely understand a section. This approach will not work for technical texts that build one concept on another, such as math or economics. In fields like those, or in foreign language studies, you must understand everything that has been discussed previously before you can master a new concept.

To increase your comprehension of the text as a whole, try to make your reading sequential. Most texts are written in this manner, but keep it in mind, especially if you are jumping from one source to another.

Periodically during your studying, review the material you have covered and test yourself on it. This is the best way for you to determine whether the information is really sinking in. If you find your comprehension of a subject isn't as good as you would like it to be, review the subject in depth.

RATE YOUR READING SPEED

To rate your speed of reading, take any text of about 200 words and read it from start to finish. Time yourself as you do so. Then score yourself as follows:

Under 25 seconds—Very fast

26–40 seconds—Fast

41–55 seconds—Average

56–70 seconds—Slow

71+ seconds—Very slow

If your reading speed falls in the slow or very slow range, you should plan to do something about it. You don't have the reading skill you need to be competitive. But be careful; trying to read faster than your normal speed may harm your reading comprehension. The following tips will help you gain speed without losing comprehension.

1. Focus your attention and give your full concentration to the material you are reading.
2. Eliminate outside distractions that might interrupt your concentration.
3. Do your reading in a comfortable environment that is conducive to study.
4. Don't worry about understanding every word in the text, but do look up words that must be understood in order for you to grasp a concept.
5. Rather than trying to understand and remember every detail, focus on forming a good understanding of the overall concepts presented in the text.

Most important is that you always read at a comfortable speed. If you find you just can't speed up your reading to the point you'd like, don't sacrifice your comprehension for speed! You'll be far better off in the long run understanding everything you've read than getting through the material a little faster.

STRATEGIES FOR READING COMPREHENSION TESTS

Few contemporary law enforcement employment exams contain trick questions. However, administrators will often phrase questions so that test takers must read carefully if they are going to select the correct answer. Reading too quickly or losing your concentration may prevent you from fully understanding a question, and thus your answer will probably be wrong. Use the following test-taking strategies to improve your reading comprehension and your score on the written portion of your police exam.

1. Read the questions before you read the text. That way you'll have an idea of what facts are important as you read; you'll save time by not having to go back to look for answers. If you find the answer as you read, underline it. If the question asks for factual information, scan the passage quickly to see if the answer "jumps out" at you before you take the time to read the entire paragraph.

2. If you're not good at "reading between the lines" to answer inference-type questions, answer the factual questions first. By the time

you're done with those questions, you will have a basic familiarity with the text and inference questions will be easier.

3. Read each question with total concentration, then rephrase it in your own words. By doing this you can be sure you totally understand what is being asked before you try to answer the question.

4. Don't jump around from one paragraph to another or from one section of the exam to another. It's okay to skip difficult questions and come back later, as discussed previously, but don't jump around in the text just because you find one topic more interesting than another. Many test sections follow a logical progression; it's important to keep your reading comprehension in sequence with the same progression.

5. Study the directions that precede test questions—simple reading is often insufficient. Reread any sentence or paragraph that you do not completely understand. Because most paragraphs and sentences in the directions build on each other, you may miss an important directive if you don't understand even one sentence.

6. If you find you lose your place when reading, hold a piece of white paper below the sentence or paragraph you are currently reading, whichever you prefer. This stops your eyes from wandering on the page and often improves your concentration and comprehension.

7. Using a pencil, underline important facts as you read and leave a question mark by any sentence to which you want to return. Use the margins to quickly summarize an idea or thought in your own words. You'll be amazed at how much easier it is to understand something expressed this way. However, be careful not to spend too much time doing this; use the technique only for those concepts that are giving you trouble.

READING COMPREHENSION SUMMARY

Definitions of Key Terms: _____
_____
_____
_____
_____

Questions That Help Clarify the Topic: _____

_____

_____

_____

_____

Questions for Which I Don't Know the Answers Yet:_____

_____

_____

_____

_____

Definitions of Key Terms: _____

_____

_____

_____

_____

Questions that Help Clarify the Topic:_____

_____

_____

_____

_____

Questions for Which I Don't Know the Answers Yet:_____

_____

_____

_____

_____

Make as many copies of this chart as you need.

QUESTIONS • COMMENTS • THINGS TO DO

STEP 13

"The empires of the future are empires of the mind."

—**Winston Churchill**

REPORT WRITING

DATE:

OBJECTIVE:

To learn how to write an effective police report.

PURPOSE:

Except for routine patrol, report writing is the single most continuous activity in which you will be engaged as a police officer. No matter what duties you fulfill during your working day, you will usually have some type of report that you must file on each incident.

Because report writing is such an important part of a police officer's job, your written exam will test you on your ability to write a clear, concise report. Today's assignment will teach you the essential components of any good police report, enabling you to pass this section of your exam with flying colors.

TIME REQUIRED: Two hours.

ASSIGNMENT:

1. Study the section titled "Components of the Police Report."
2. Complete the report-writing exercise.

COMPONENTS OF THE POLICE REPORT

Being able to write well may be considered the single most important skill in today's workplace. A worker who is a good writer will often make career advances much more quickly than a worker who is a poor writer but whose skills are otherwise equal. This is especially, though not exclusively, true in jobs that require the worker to write on a regular basis.

Writing is a very important aspect of a police officer's job. You will be required to write reports on a daily basis. You will also be tested on your ability to piece together a good police report before you are offered a position, so it is important that you understand the basics before you enter the exam.

This text is not designed to teach you in-depth writing skills. If you feel you have deficiencies in that area, you might consider taking a course that specializes in teaching writing skills. However, by understanding what should be included in a written police report, you will be prepared to answer these questions effectively on your police exam.

Three Components

A written police report consists of the following three components:

1. Accurate and thorough recording of all basic factual information. This includes names, addresses, phone numbers, street names, time of day, car license plates, etc.
2. Accurate and thorough recording of investigative information. This category includes descriptions of actions taken, decisions made, inferences drawn, etc.
3. Format. This category is concerned with the overall organization of your report. Did you properly organize all the information so that the end result is clear, logical and easy to read? Did you enter appropriate headings? Is every relevant category of information included?

Your report will be judged in each of these three areas. Note that all three work together to form the final product; none is sufficient unto itself. Thus the best-written report will not be adequate if it does not contain all the basic information of the case. Likewise, the report writer who has captured every detail of an incident but whose organization is choppy and confusing will not receive a high score. Be sure you give careful consideration to each basic category as you write your report.

Information to Include

In previous sections we have discussed the importance of NEOTWY: when, where, who, what, how, and why. Make sure you consider each of these as you complete your report; no report is complete without some accounting for each topic.

A common mistake made by new officers is always applying NEOTWY in a fixed order without giving consideration to the flow and logical sequence of the report. Consider the following example, in which all information is presented in the order mandated by the memory device NEOTWY.

It was 9:15 A.M. (when) at the corner of Vine and Main streets (where). The suspect, Albert Jones (who) was apprehended for assault with a deadly weapon—a knife (what). Police were called in by a local store owner who witnessed the incident (how). The suspect had attempted to rob a pedestrian but became upset when the man refused to give up his wallet, and that was when he pulled out the knife (why)."

Now consider the following report. It contains the same information, but is reorganized to be more logical and easier to read.

"At 9:15 A.M. (when) a call was received from a local store owner (how), notifying police of an incident taking place at the corner of Vine and Main streets (where). Police arrived at the scene to find a pedestrian being threatened by a man with a knife (what). After being taken into custody, the perpetrator, Albert Jones (who), made the statement that he had attempted to rob the pedestrian but had become upset and pulled his knife when the man refused to give up his wallet (why)."

Do you see the difference? Although the information given in the two reports is identical, the second report describes the events in a logical sequence, whereas the order of events in the first report is not sequential. Always make sure your written reports read logically. Just this one step will improve your score on this section of your written exam. Also keep the following points in mind when writing a police report.

- Use commonly understood words. There's no reason to use a big word where a small one will do. Use technical terms only when necessary.
- Use the active voice. It's much more effective to say "The perpetrator shot the passerby" than "The passerby was shot by the perpetrator."
- Sentences should be short and direct. Omit needless words. Revise sentence structure if needed to accomplish this.

- Keep paragraphs short.
- Use headings, topic sentences, and summarizing sentences where appropriate. It will help the overall organization of your report.
- Itemize to call attention to specific information. For example, you might write the following:

  Items found in the suspect's car included

  > 4 beer cans
  >
  > 14 teddy bears
  >
  > 8 t-shirts

- Use specific and concrete wording rather than generalized and abstract wording.

EXERCISE—REPORT WRITING

Using the facts below, write a short report describing the incident.

Name of suspect:	John M. Smith
Age of suspect:	23
Address of suspect:	240 Clark Street, Big Town
Date:	February 7, 2001
Time:	7:08 P.M.
Location:	Maple Street parking lot
Offense:	Auto theft
Witnesses:	Jane Doe
Arresting officer:	Bob Jones, badge #3095

_____

_____

_____

_____

_____

_____

_____

_____

_____

_____

_____

_____

_____

_____

_____

_____

_____

_____

_____

_____

_____

_____

_____

QUESTIONS • COMMENTS • THINGS TO DO

STEP

14

HANDLE MAP QUESTIONS AND SEND TEN COVER LETTERS AND RESUMES

DATE:

OBJECTIVE:

To learn to understand and clearly describe directional maps and to send ten cover letters and resumes.

PURPOSE:

The ability to understand and clearly describe maps may be useful during your police employment exam. Often the written exam will include questions that present you with a map, then ask you to choose the best route to a location. Today's assignment gives you tips you will find useful in answering these questions.

Your chances of landing that law enforcement job are increasing with each resume you send out!

TIME REQUIRED: Three hours.

ASSIGNMENTS:

1. Read the section titled "Answering Map Questions."
2. Answer sample exam questions.
3. Send out ten cover letters and resumes.

SEND TEN RESUMES AND COVER LETTERS

Record below the names of the agencies you contact.

1. _____
2. _____
3. _____
4. _____
5. _____
6. _____
7. _____
8. _____
9. _____
10. _____

ANSWERING MAP QUESTIONS

The ability to answer questions based on directional maps builds on a skill discussed earlier—evaluating visual information. Apply the techniques you learned in earlier assignments to begin your understanding of maps. Look over the entire map, then move on to examining successively smaller and smaller details until you feel confident you can begin to answer the questions.

When evaluating a map, trace each potential route before selecting your answers. You may think you have seen every possible alternative, but you may be surprised at how much more you will see when you actually take your pencil and block out each route. Doing this will also ensure that you don't forget the routes you identified as the test goes along. Be sure you count the number of turns taken by each route; that is one of the strongest indications of the best way to travel.

Be especially careful to identify one-way streets and circle or highlight them if necessary. It is easy, when rushed, to select a route that looks quickest but takes you the wrong way down a one-way street.

The following map and subsequent questions are very similar to those you will face during actual employment examinations.

SAMPLE MAP QUESTIONS

In the map below, the arrow symbol is used to represent the direction of the flow of traffic. Study the map, then answer the questions that follow. You may examine the map as often as necessary when answering the questions. Note that the police station on this map is located in the bottom left-hand corner.

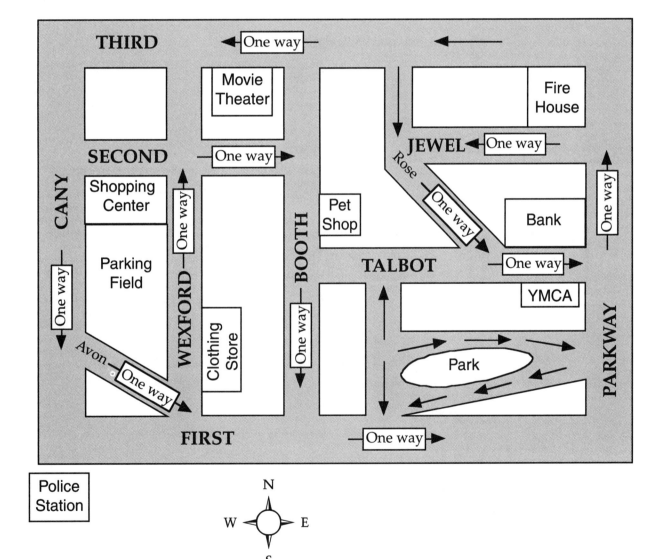

QUESTIONS

1. Your patrol car is sent from the police station to the pet shop on Talbot. The shortest way to get there without breaking the law is to go
   A. east on First, north on Booth, right on Talbot
   B. north on Cany, right on Second, right on Booth, left on Talbot
   C. east on First, north on Wexford, right on Second, right on Booth, left on Talbot

2. Your patrol car at the pet shop is sent to the movie theater on Third. The shortest way to get there without breaking the law is to go
   A. east on Talbot, northwest on Rose, left on Third
   B. east on Talbot, north on Parkway, left on Jewel, right on Rose, left on Third
   C. east on Talbot, south on Parkway, west on First, north on Wexford, east on Third
   D. east on Talbot, north on Parkway, west on Third

3. Your patrol car at the movie theater is sent to the fire house on Parkway. The shortest way to get there without breaking the law is to go
   A. west on Third, south on Cany, east on Second, south on Booth, east on Talbot, north on Parkway
   B. west on Third, left on Wexford, left on First, north on Parkway
   C. west on Third, south on Cany, east on First, north on Parkway
   D. west on Third, south on Cany, left on Avon, east on First, north on Parkway

4. Your patrol car at the fire house is sent to the YMCA by the oval park. What is the shortest way to get there without breaking the law? Write it in the space provided.

   _____

   _____

Answers: 1–C; 2–D; 3–A; 4—West on Third, south and then southeast on Rose; 5—North on Parkway, west on Third, south on Cany, east on First, north on Wexford

5. Your patrol car at the YMCA is sent to the clothing store on Wexford. What is the shortest way to get there without breaking the law? Write it in the space provided.

_____

_____

QUESTIONS • COMMENTS • THINGS TO DO

STEP 15

"He who has done his best for his own time has lived for all times."

—Johann Von Schiller

ACING JOB INTERVIEWS

DATE:

OBJECTIVE:

To learn what situations you can expect to encounter in a job interview, and to master the techniques that will ensure that you make a great impression—every time.

PURPOSE:

A job interview is a meeting between an employer and a job candidate. Its primary purpose is for the employer to determine whether a certain candidate matches the company's needs, although it also gives the candidate the opportunity to evaluate the company according to his or her needs and wants.

It is very important that you understand the format of job interviews so you can be prepared for anything. Knowing what to expect will allow you to prepare for your interview, thus increasing your interview effectiveness and generating more job offers.

TIME REQUIRED: Four hours.

ASSIGNMENTS:

1. Study the section titled "Understanding the Job Interview."
2. Practice and improve your interview skills by answering the sample questions in this section.

UNDERSTANDING THE JOB INTERVIEW

The job interview is the biggest hurdle you will have to overcome in your job search. Unlike the police exam, which is an objective measure of your skills and knowledge, an interview is largely subjective. Although your experience and skills are important, it is equally important that you make a good impression on the interviewer. If you seem unfriendly, unprepared, or unprofessional, the job will probably go to someone else, no matter how impressive your qualifications.

Luckily, it is possible to prepare for the job interview. By knowing what kinds of questions you are likely to be asked, knowing what is necessary to make a good impression, and being able to recognize the most common interview traps, you can perform impressively in any interview.

There are two types of job interviews for which you must prepare: the initial screening interview and the selection interview.

The Initial Screening Interview

The screening interview is a brief meeting or phone call between an employer and a job candidate to determine whether a candidate meets the department's criteria; its purpose is to screen candidates out. It's certainly not fair that highly qualified candidates may be turned down based on a 15-minute conversation, but agencies often receive so many applications for one job opening that there is no other efficient way to narrow the field. Your only goal in this type of interview is to avoid being screened out.

Because the screening interview is so short and superficial, it is absolutely essential that you make a good impression. Greet the interviewer with a friendly smile and a firm handshake, and make a mental note of his or her name so you can use it during the interview.

Before you go to the interview, do your homework. Find out some information about the agency by doing research in the library or by calling and talking to an employee. Then make sure you demonstrate your knowledge to the interviewer. It may be appropriate to do this in a strong initiating statement, or you may prefer to wait until you are given the opening by the interviewer. You will almost always be asked some form of the question, "What do you know about our police department?" early in the interview. Not only will your knowledge impress the interviewer, it will also give you information that will help you make a decision about whether the department is right for you.

Above all, be confident. An interview is not the place for false modesty or timidity. Always remember that if the employer didn't think you had the skills to perform the job for which you are being interviewed, he or she wouldn't be talking to you at all. Your confidence is reassuring to the interviewer; not only does your résumé indicate that you can handle the job, so does your attitude.

The interviewer will run through your qualifications briefly to make sure you are indeed qualified for the job being offered, but won't delve very deep in the screening interview. If you have made a good first impression, one that projects confidence, enthusiasm, and interest, the interviewer has probably already made up his or her mind that you are a strong candidate who is worth talking to at greater length.

The Selection Interview

Once you've made the cut, you may be asked to return for a more in-depth selection interview, if the department doesn't have an oral board. Unlike the screening interview, which seeks to screen out less qualified applicants, the selection interview aims to choose the best person from a field of acceptable candidates. You will be judged in seven areas: the impression you make, communication skills, enthusiasm, leadership, competence, job history, and interest in the job being offered.

TYPES OF QUESTIONS

Be ready to answer three types of questions: closed, open-ended, and probing. Listen carefully to all questions and don't rush your responses. Keep the interviewer's selection criteria in mind throughout the interview and gear your answers toward satisfying him or her that you amply meet all the department's requirements.

Closed Questions

Closed questions are straightforward and easy to answer. The interviewer often needs to gather some basic information and will ask simple factual questions. Your job is to make your answers as conversational and friendly as possible, and to inject any information that reflects positively on your attitude or experience. For instance, an interviewer will usually ask, "When can you start?" Instead of replying "Two weeks," a standard answer and one the interviewer expects, you might say, "I would appreciate being able to give two weeks to my present employer in order to help ease the transition. I wouldn't want to leave my company in a bind. Does that time frame work for you?" This reply indicates professionalism and loyalty on the part of the job candidate and makes a great impression.

Open-Ended Questions

Open-ended questions are broad in scope and give the candidate great flexibility in response. Questions such as "Tell me a little about yourself" demand that the candidate choose exactly what information to reveal; no specifics are requested.

Open-ended questions can be a blessing or a curse, depending on how you handle them. You can take the opportunity to prove your strengths over and over again to the interviewer, or you can hang yourself with the rope these questions provide by answering in an uncertain, disorganized manner that doesn't show your skills in their best light. Too many candidates respond to open-ended questions with irrelevant or nondirected statements. A good response provides positive information that gives the applicant an outstanding rating in one of the seven categories discussed earlier.

Probing Questions

A probing question lies somewhere between a closed and an open-ended question. It gives the applicant some flexibility of response, but asks for specific facts, such as the reason the applicant did something. Probing questions indicate that the interviewer is not yet completely satisfied with the information he or she has been given; more information is needed. The applicant's job is to determine whether the interviewer is trying to verify a strength or a weakness, and to reply accordingly. Use your response to prove that you have the required strengths or to ease the interviewer's concern about a perceived liability.

Preparation is the key to success in this area. On the next page is a list of some of the most common open-ended and probing questions you can expect to encounter in an interview.

Common Open-Ended Interview Questions

1. Tell me a little about yourself.
2. Why should we hire you?
3. Tell me about your work experience.
4. What interests you most about this job?
5. Discuss some of the things that are most important to you in a job.
6. What is your ideal job?
7. How can you contribute to our department?
8. What motivates you?
9. Do you feel you have management potential? If so, why?
10. What is your greatest accomplishment?
11. What is your greatest strength?
12. What is your greatest weakness?
13. What is the job accomplishment you are most proud of?
14. What is the biggest mistake you have ever made?
15. What have you learned from your failures or mistakes?
16. What are your short-term goals?
17. What are your long-term goals (where do you want to be 5, 10, 15 years from now)?
18. What do you consider success to be?
19. What makes you better than the other candidates I've interviewed for this position?
20. What other skills do you have that would be useful in this position?

Common Probing Interview Questions

1. How well do you handle stress?
2. Why are you leaving your current employer after only a year?
3. Why are you seeking a career change?
4. Why are you interested in this position?
5. What other departments are you considering?
6. Why have you been unemployed for so long?
7. What did you dislike about your previous employer?
8. What did you think of your last boss?
9. Do you consider yourself to be a creative person?
10. Do you prefer to work alone or with others?
11. Are you good with people?

12. What are your feelings about job-related travel?
13. Are you in good health?
14. Do you have any hobbies or special interests?
15. What makes you think you will be a good supervisor?

INTERVIEWING TECHNIQUES

A good interviewer knows what to look for, and if he or she is having trouble gathering the information needed—whether the candidate is being deliberately evasive or just missing the point of the question—various techniques will be employed to get to that information.

Repeat Questions. This is just what it sounds like. An interviewer who has not gotten a satisfying answer to a question may ask the same question later in the interview. Often the interviewer feels that a rapport has been established during the course of the interview, and that the applicant may be comfortable enough late in the interview to give a more truthful or complete answer to the question the second time around. The interviewer may also be checking for consistency.

Stick to your guns! Be consistent in your answers; inconsistency will always make a bad impression. This holds true for multiple interviews as well. Don't assume that two interviewers won't compare notes. They probably will, and it's likely that your inconsistency will come to light.

Looping Back. This technique is used when the interviewer believes that the applicant is not telling the whole story. Perhaps the more the applicant is questioned, the vaguer and more evasive he or she becomes. The interviewer may drop the subject for the moment but return to it later by a different route, attempting to get at the same information by using a totally different approach.

For instance, an applicant may claim to be very familiar with a computer program he has really only used once or twice. During questioning, the interviewer notices that there are curious gaps in the applicant's knowledge. The more the interviewer presses, the more evasive the applicant becomes. Seeming to drop the subject, the interviewer moves on to other topics. However, later in the interview the applicant may be told he will be required to take a test on the software in question. Whether or not the interviewer actually intends to make the applicant take the test, you can bet the applicant's response to this statement will be carefully noted!

As with repeat questions, the key to handling looping questions is consistency. Be wary of seemingly innocent questions that seek to catch you off guard.

Requesting Specifics. Many otherwise strong job applicants can be tripped up by this technique. Imagine you have prepared for your interview and when you are asked the question, "What is your strongest skill?" you know exactly what to say. You reel off your prepared answer, and then the interviewer hits you with the whammy. "Can you give me several specific examples of how this skill has impacted your job performance in the past?" No matter how honest your first answer was, the second question can make you seem insincere if you're not prepared with facts and figures. You must always be able to back up your statements.

Be prepared. When studying the open-ended and probing questions presented earlier, take the time to think about any specific examples you could use to back up your answers.

CLOSING THE INTERVIEW

During most interviews, the interviewer gives the applicant an overview of the agency and the job being offered. At the end of the interview, the applicant will usually be asked if he or she has any questions about the job or the agency. It is expected that you will have questions; the most common applicant response, that the interviewer has provided so much information that the applicant has no questions at all, indicates a lack of preparation and interest.

Note that this is not the time to ask questions about benefits, holidays, etc.; that is best done after a formal job offer is made. Rather, you are seeking information about the agency and the job. Remember, whether or not you go to work for any law enforcement agency is not only the agencies choice. It's yours, too, and you must make sure a job is right for you.

Sample Applicant Questions

1. What are the major responsibilities of this position?
2. Why is this position vacant?

3. Where would I fit in on the organizational chart?
4. What are the strengths of your agency?
5. How many sworn officers are there?
6. To whom would I report?
7. Does your agency encourage employee initiative?
8. Is there room for growth?
9. What are the major priorities of this position?

Finally, make sure you exit the interview with the same strong, confident manner you've maintained throughout. Don't allow your enthusiasm, poise, and self-confidence to flag at all. Repeat the handshake and smile you gave the interviewer at the beginning and make a strong closing statement. Saying "Thank you" and leaving isn't enough. Instead, say something like, "Thank you very much for meeting with me, Ms. Jones. After talking with you and learning a little about the requirements of this job, I feel even more confident that I am qualified for the job you are offering, and that I can do an excellent job for you. I look forward to hearing from you." By doing this, you leave the interviewer with the impression that you are ready, willing, and able to take over the job. He or she can't help but be impressed.

The Thank-You Letter

Sit down immediately after the interview and write a brief note to the interviewer thanking him or her again for the time spent with you and reaffirming your belief that you are qualified for the job. Put it in the mail the same day, if possible. Your follow-up will be impressive and will ensure that your name stays firmly in the interviewer's mind.

REVIEWING THE INTERVIEW

Jot down a few notes after each interview. Reviewing your notes before each new interview will remind you of the areas in which you had trouble and will ensure that you don't fall into the same traps twice.

Actual question: _____

_____

What did they really want to know? _____

_____

Answer I gave: _____

_____

Points to include next time: _____

_____

_____

_____

Actual question: _____

_____

What did they really want to know?

_____

Answer I gave: _____

_____

Points to include next time: _____

_____

_____

_____

Actual question: _____

_____

What did they really want to know? _____

_____

Answer given: _____

_____

Points to include next time: _____

_____

_____

QUESTIONS • COMMENTS • THINGS TO DO

STEP

16

"What the superior man seeks is in himself; what the small man seeks is in others."

—François la Rochefoucauld

ORAL BOARDS—PART I AND SEND TEN COVER LETTERS/RESUMES

DATE:

OBJECTIVE:

To learn the basic format of an oral board and obtain the skills you will need to perform well and to send ten cover letters and resumes.

PURPOSE:

The oral board is the single most important part of the law enforcement employment process. It is during this 20- to 40-minute period that those making the employment decisions form concrete impressions or confirm prior decisions about who should be hired and who should not. Candidates who fail the interview are not placed on the eligibility list; those who score above the cutoff are placed on the list in rank order by numerical score. The better you do on the oral board, the higher your name is on the list and the more likely it is that you will be hired.

Today's assignment will teach you what to expect in your oral board and how to prepare for it. As always, preparation is the key to success. By following the strategies listed in this section you will be able to ace your oral board.

By sending out ten more cover letters and resumes, you're getting your name out to more and more potential employers.

TIME REQUIRED: Four hours.

ASSIGNMENTS:

1. Read the section titled "An Overview of the Oral Board."
2. Complete the "So What?" exercise.
3. Send out ten cover letters and resumes.

AN OVERVIEW OF THE ORAL BOARD

As stated earlier, the oral board is the most important part of the law enforcement application process. No matter how well you do on your written exam, a poor performance on your oral board will take you out of the running for a police job.

Because the oral board is so important, it is easy to allow yourself to feel an enormous amount of stress about it. However, you may also choose not to feel stress. That's easier said than done, of course. But with proper preparation and knowing what to expect, your level of confidence will be high enough that you will be able to view the oral board process as a personal challenge. Expect to do exceptionally well on your oral board and you probably will.

The more stress and pressure interviewers throw at you, the more confidence you must radiate back. There is pressure in every interview situation, but you must be prepared to show that you can handle it. Be decisive in developing your answers to questions; use logical justification to support your point of view.

THE RATING SYSTEM

The oral board is designed to measure four dimensions: job preparation, interpersonal ability, decision-making ability, and verbal communication skills. Materials consist of a candidate rating form, a set of rating scales, and a final rating form. One rating scale is included for each dimension being rated; each scale states the definition of the dimension and sets forth rating scale descriptions. At the end of the interview, all four scores are combined to produce the candidate's total score.

Each dimension is assigned a relative weight by subject matter experts; the sum of all four dimensions is 100%. It is recommended, but not required, that dimension weights be used during scoring. You will not know the weights of each section, however. Just remember that to do as well as possible, you must treat every dimension as being equally important.

TYPES OF QUESTIONS

You will probably be asked two types of questions in the oral board: situational and general. The general questions are broad interview questions of the type discussed in the section on preparing for the job interview. They involve your relevant education and experience, training, job understanding, and job preparation. Situational questions ask the candidate to describe his or her response to an imagined situation. The response is judged by how close it comes to describing "ideal" behavior in the given situation.

The same set of general and situational questions is asked of all candidates in order to make the comparison process as fair as possible.

One of the most important questions you will be asked is, "Why should we hire you?" Be very well prepared to answer it. This question is a golden opportunity, an invitation for you to show the interviewers exactly why they should hire you. Your answer should cover all the relevant areas:

1. Your desire to make substantial contributions to the organization
2. Your eagerness to accept the challenges of the job
3. Your education and work credentials
4. Your desire to succeed within the agency
5. Your enthusiasm and sincerity

On the other hand, you may be asked some questions that have no clear correct answer. If so, understand that the point of these questions is to see how well you handle a stressful, difficult situation. The interviewer is watching to see how you react. He or she wants to see if you can maintain your composure and think effectively under stress.

If you find a question impossible to answer, simply state that you feel unqualified to answer it. Don't try to portray yourself as knowing the answers to every question; you're not expected to know everything and acting as if you do may hurt you more than it will help you. Have a realistic understanding of your abilities and inabilities, and don't be afraid to be human during the interview. However, don't use this "out" too often; use it only on questions that you simply cannot answer. Some questions will ask for judgment calls, and though you may not be sure what answer the interviewer is looking for, you still need to demonstrate your common sense and ability to think on your feet.

CHOOSING YOUR WORDS

Your answers to boring questions can come alive if you use the right responses. Learn how to paint pictures with descriptive, action-oriented statements. This is called the "so what?" strategy. Once you understand and practice this strategy, it will become easy and natural.

Look at the following chart. On the left-hand side, under the heading "Achievement," write a sentence or two that describes a personal achievement or accomplishment. An example might be, "I played basketball in college." Now on the right side under the heading "So What?" describe what's so great about the statement you made on the left. A good answer in this case would be something like, "Being in great shape will be very beneficial in my law enforcement career."

Achievement	So What?

If an interviewer says, "Tell me something about yourself and what you've been doing," you must be prepared. This is an example of a situation in which the "So what?" strategy will be effective. Each time you make a statement, ask yourself, "So what?" The answers you reach in your head can then be incorporated into the statement to make your answer more impressive.

Your goal during the oral board, as in any interview, is to turn positive background information into even greater assets and to turn negative facts into positives. For instance, "I quit college after two and a half years and never received my degree" is a negative statement. The same situation could be more positively expressed like this: "Even though family-related circumstances required that I pursue a full-time career before I received my degree, I've always continued my education through work-related courses and seminars."

If you can avoid talking about your weaknesses, you should do so at all costs. However, you will probably be asked about your weaknesses, and you need to be prepared to answer the question in a positive manner. Before you enter the interview, give a great deal of thought to your personal strengths and weaknesses. Then wipe the word "weakness" from your vocabulary. To be really good during oral boards you must not perceive yourself as having weaknesses; instead, consider them to be merely "areas that need improvement." This type of thinking will improve your self-image, your attitude, and your professional appearance.

When talking about areas that need improvement, always mention how you are working on correcting the situation. A crucial element in your answer is the manner in which you field the question. Keep the "need improvement" areas focused on professional concerns; avoid bringing up personal topics. They're not relevant to your job application, but may reflect negatively on you.

SEND TEN COVER LETTERS AND RESUMES

Record below the names of the agencies you contact.

1. _____
2. _____
3. _____
4. _____
5. _____
6. _____
7. _____
8. _____
9. _____
10. _____

QUESTIONS • COMMENTS • THINGS TO DO

"All great achievements require time."

—David Joseph Schwartz

POLICE ORAL BOARD QUESTIONS

DATE:

OBJECTIVE:

To become proficient in answering the questions most commonly asked in police oral boards.

PURPOSE:

By organizing your answers to the following questions before you enter your oral board, you will be fully prepared to handle any question, general or situational, that the interviewers can throw at you. Your preparation and the confidence it gives you will be very impressive to the interviewers!

TIME REQUIRED: Three hours.

ASSIGNMENTS:

1. Review the sample situational questions and correct answers included in this section.
2. Review the list of general questions you are likely to be asked and prepare your answers.

ORAL BOARDS—SAMPLE SITUATIONAL QUESTIONS

Situational questions are designed to test your judgment and your ability to stand up to stress. The following twenty questions will give you a good idea of the kinds of questions you may be asked. Try them out; use your common sense. After you try to answer the questions yourself, read the answers given by experienced police officers and see how close you come. Study the answers. They cover a broad range of police procedure that you should know in order to be good at answering situational questions.

1. You are a new officer, just out of the police academy. You're teamed with an older and experienced officer. What if your partner suggests that you get a free meal at a restaurant? What if he's going to rate your performance as an officer-on-probation?

2. A drunk is weaving his way down the side of a highway. He's singing a song. What do you do? What if he starts cursing you? What if he's 6′4″ and built like an ox? What if you're alone?

3. You see a car cross over a double yellow line, and a second car traveling in the opposite direction hits it. The driver of the first car asks, "Did you see how fast the other guy was going?" What do you do?

4. Your sergeant explains a police procedure to a group of you, but you're not sure that you understand. What do you do? What if you still don't understand the instructions after he goes over them again?

5. You see a speeding car and flag it down. As you approach the driver you see that it's your supervising sergeant. What do you do? What if the driver is the commanding officer of your precinct? What if the driver is your own mother?

6. You are driving on patrol and someone runs out to the middle of the street. He tells you that his father suffered a heart attack. What do you do? Suppose he has already called for an ambulance and has been waiting for 20 minutes? a half-hour? an hour?

7. You are speeding on your way to assist an officer when you see a bad accident. What do you do? Suppose two people are very seriously injured. What do you do?

8. Suppose you are giving a parking ticket to a pretty (or handsome) driver who starts making advances to you. You are extremely attracted to the person. What do you do? What if he or

she gives you a phone number (or asks for yours) and suggests you get together?

9. You see a well-dressed man urinating next to a parked car. No one else is around. What do you do? What if people are driving by and he is in plain sight? What if he says that he was caught in a traffic jam and couldn't wait?

10. You hear what sounds like a gunshot. You see a group of people, some adult and some teenagers. What do you do? What if someone says, "You got a search warrant? No? Well, then, get the hell out of here!"

11. You stop a car going approximately 65 miles per hour and the driver says, "You're a lazy SOB, doing nothing better than giving people tickets. I was going okay and no one else is on the highway. What's the big deal?" Suppose the driver refuses to give you his license?

12. You see two people fighting and a large crowd is around them. As you wade through the crowd, someone throws a racial slur at you—"nigger" or "honkie" or "wetback." What do you do? What if they spit at you? Or block your path? Or push you around?

13. You are given a call to investigate a noisy party. The participants want you to join the party. What do you do?

14. You are on patrol in a "white" area and see two black men taking parts off a parked car. What do you do?

15. You are called to break up a fight in a bar. There are two men engaged in a fist fight. What do you do?

16. An elderly lady calls to complain about some teenagers playing in the street in front of her house. What do you do? Suppose they don't listen to you?

17. You are on patrol and see a man running out of a jewelry store with a gun. He is chasing a group of teenagers with knives. What do you do? Suppose the man shoots and wounds one of the teenagers. What do you do?

18. You see a house on fire and someone carrying a gasoline can running away. What do you do?

19. You see a young woman acting strange. She is sitting and waving her hands in the air. What do you do? What if she gets violent as you near her? What if the other officers have accused you of asking for help too often?

20. A man hits and seriously injures a young girl with his car. You handcuff him and take him to your car. The crowd wants to beat him up and surrounds you. What do you do?

ANSWERS FOR SAMPLE SITUATIONAL QUESTIONS

1. I would just go along with it, because he's the senior officer and is supposed to be training me. I would decide for myself, though, that it was an unethical procedure and that I wouldn't do it once I had a choice in the matter.

2. I would stop and get him off the highway (or street if he's walking) and take him into custody for his own safety and the safety of others. If he started cursing me I'd just ignore him and proceed. It wouldn't matter how he was built, either; size shouldn't come into the picture. The police have to deal with all types of people and be prepared to handle situations like this alone, because you won't always be with a partner. So regardless of his size, I'd just proceed.

3. The accident happened because the first guy went over the line and into the other lane. He would get a ticket for this, and I would tell him that he was the cause of the accident, not the guy speeding. I would also tell him that I didn't know how fast the other guy was going; I probably wouldn't.

4. I would ask him to explain it further. If I was still the only one who didn't understand, I would wait until after the line-up and go up to him and ask him to explain it again.

5. I would explain to him that I stopped him because he was speeding, in case he didn't understand. I would not give him a ticket. If the driver were my mother I would do the same thing, only I would give her a lecture about her careless driving. If it were the commanding officer of my station, again, I would let him go.

6. I would get headquarters on the phone and alert them to the situation so that they could send an ambulance. Then I would grab the oxygen tank from the trunk and follow the person to where his father was. I would keep the man on oxygen or perform CPR if necessary. If they had already called an ambulance, then the one I called would be a back-up in case the first one was delayed.

7. I would stop at the accident to see if anyone was injured. If someone was, I would notify headquarters to send an ambulance. If the accident was serious I would stay on the scene and tell headquarters to get another back-up for the incident I was going to in the first place. At the accident I have a known life-threatening situation, so I have to stay there instead of pro-

ceeding to a possible life-threatening situation. If the accident was minor, though, I'd have the ambulance notified and go to assist the other officer. Then I'd have headquarters send someone else to handle the accident and write up the report.

8. I would give the person the ticket anyway, then take the phone number and follow up when I was off duty.

9. If no one else was around I would give him a verbal reprimand and inform him that his actions were against the law. If there were people around, I would arrest him as a disorderly person. How he was dressed had nothing to do with it, and if he was stuck, tough, because you just don't urinate in public like that.

10. First, I would find out if it really was a gunshot. This could be done simply by judging the temperament of the crowd. If they were restless and scurrying about, I would immediately notify headquarters of the situation. But if everyone was standing around casually, it may well have been a firecracker or something similar. I would approach the adults, though, and ask what was going on before I called it in. If some guy verbally harassed me I would get his identification and handle it from there. If he started to get physical I might have to arrest him, or if it was really a gunshot and he was trying to interfere with my investigation I might have grounds to arrest him.

11. I would give him a ticket for going 65 mph. If he refused to surrender his license, I'd arrest him. It's possible he doesn't even have a license.

12. I'd ignore the racial slurs and arrest the men for fighting. If they started to push me around, I'd radio for some back-up help. I'm not sure I should try to handle an unruly crowd alone.

13. I would investigate the situation. If everything was okay besides the noise, I'd simply tell them to turn down the music because they're disturbing the peace. I'd tell them to have a good time, but I wouldn't join the party.

14. I would question them and see if they had a registration for the car. If they didn't, I would try to find and question the car owner to see if they had permission to be working on the car.

15. I would arrest both men for fighting, but would try to have a partner before walking into a crowd situation.

16. I'd check out the situation. If they were rowdy I'd tell them to keep it down. If they didn't listen, I'd put them in the car and take them home.

17. I'd radio headquarters right away. I'd attempt to get everyone to stop and drop their weapons. If they didn't, I'd pursue them. If the man hit one of the boys, I'd order him to drop his gun. If he didn't, I'd shoot at the man. He is in the wrong because his life is not being threatened and he does not have the right to fire his gun, especially in public where he could hurt an innocent bystander.

18. First, I'd make sure there was no one in the house after making a mental picture of the man. It's more important to save lives than to effect an arrest.

19. I would stop and ask the woman if she was all right. I'd look into the situation further if she got violent. I'd try to restrain her and find out what's making her act that way. Perhaps she's suffering from insulin withdrawal, or maybe it's more serious, like a narcotic overdose.

20. I would immediately call headquarters for assistance. I don't feel I could do much alone in a mob scene. I would call an ambulance for the girl and then do my best to protect the criminal by getting him into the car and away from the scene as soon as possible.

ORAL BOARDS—SAMPLE GENERAL QUESTIONS

Use the following questions to help you prepare for your oral board.

1. Why are you interested in law enforcement as a career?
2. What have you done to prepare yourself for a career in law enforcement?
3. What personal qualities do you think you have that would make you a good police officer?
4. What do you perceive to be the most important function of a police officer?
5. Why have you applied for a police officer's position with the city of _____?
6. Why should we hire you over all the other candidates for this position?
7. What would you like to be doing five years from now?
8. Do you have any prejudices?
9. What is your greatest attribute?
10. How do you feel about taking a life?

11. Do you have any questions to ask the board?
12. Would you like to have the job of detective? Why?
13. Are you willing to work anywhere in the police department?
14. What are your greatest accomplishments in the past three years?
15. Do you have any plans to continue your education? What is your level of education?
16. What specific training and qualifications do you have to become a police officer?
17. What kind of experience do you have for this position?
18. What are the reasons for your success?
19. What specific traits do you have to offer?
20. How does your family feel about you becoming a police officer?
21. How much time are you willing to give to becoming a successful officer?
22. Have you ever had to discipline or fire anyone?
23. How long will you stay with the department?
24. Have you always done the best work of which you are capable?
25. How do you feel about a male (female) supervisor?
26. What kinds of decisions are most difficult for you?
27. Who has had the greatest influence on your career?
28. What causes you to become angry?
29. What would your boss tell me about you?
30. How much discretion should a police officer have in the everyday exercise of his/her authority and responsibility?
31. Should police officers be expected to have a higher standard of conduct than other members of the community?
32. How many days have you called in sick during the past year?
33. If I told you I wanted a police officer who presented a proper role model, what does that mean to you?
34. What is probable cause?
35. Name one United States Supreme Court justice.
36. What is the Bill of Rights?
37. What does the fourth amendment mean to you?
38. Would you shoot to kill or shoot to wound an armed suspect?
39. How will shift work affect your life?
40. Would you fire a warning shot?
41. How would you react if you were told you had to stay late an hour before you were due to get off work?

42. What does community policing mean to you?
43. In your opinion, does a police officer spend more time fighting crime or surveying the community?
44. How would you feel about working for someone younger than you?
45. What is the difference between the "spirit of the law" and the "letter of the law?"
46. How do you feel about female officers and minority officers?
47. How do you prefer to work? Alone or with someone?
48. What is the chain of command?
49. What does excessive force mean to you?
50. What does escalation of force mean to you?
51. Have you ever been found guilty of any law violations other than parking tickets?
52. Have you ever used illegal drugs?
53. Do you drink alcohol? How much?
54. Have you ever been reprimanded or subjected to disciplinary action?
55. Have you ever been late for work?

QUESTIONS • COMMENTS • THINGS TO DO

STEP
18

"The intensity of your desire governs the power with which the force is directed."

—John McDonald

ROLE PLAYING

DATE:

OBJECTIVE:

To practice answering oral board-type questions in a role playing situation.

PURPOSE:

No matter how much thought you have given to the questions listed earlier in this book, you will not be completely prepared for your oral board if you don't practice answering them out loud and in front of people, since this is what will be required of you during your oral board. Today's assignments will teach you role-playing techniques that will enable you to prepare for anything an interviewer can ask you.

TIME REQUIRED: Three hours.

ASSIGNMENTS:

1. Study the role playing transcript.
2. Study the section titled "Preparation Makes Perfect."
3. Using the questions from earlier sections, practice role playing techniques until you feel comfortable with your answers to all the questions.

ROLE PLAYING TRANSCRIPT

In an oral board there will be three, four, or even five interviewers, and they will not be cutting you any slack. It's the interviewers' job to put you under stress and judge how you react.

Below is a transcript of an actual oral board situation. It will give you an idea of the kind of pressure you will be under in your oral board. For the exercise to work best, put yourself in the situation; form a mental picture of four or five police officers firing questions at you as fast as they can.

"OK, you're on your way to a robbery alarm, the alert tone just went off. The tone just went off. You're down the street, you're going down the street. It's a 23 & 0, a bank alarm—an armed robbery alarm to a bank, in progress, on a crowded Friday afternoon.

"You're traveling down the street. Do you use your lights and siren? (No) You don't? Okay, what do you do when you come to the intersection? There's traffic going by in the intersection. Should you "break" the intersection? Do you go through? Do you stop the cars? Do you go through the red light? What do you do?. . . What do you do? . . . WHAT DO YOU DO?

"Forget that. You're still going, you're now nearing the bank. You're about three blocks away from the bank. Your dispatcher radios back, there's another alert tone. It is an actual armed robbery in progress at the bank. It's an actual armed robbery, it's not just an alarm. There are two white male perpetrators, one of them with a shotgun, one of them with a revolver. They're in the bank, it's going down right now.

"You're now a block away. A fellow officer is coming in on the other side. You both come in the back of the bank. You're in the parking lot. You park your car, you get out of your car. He's got a shotgun. You get your shotgun. You're at one corner of the bank, your fellow officer is at the other. You crouch down like you should, you look around the corner.

"Your fellow officer went out too far. The guys robbing the bank come out of the bank. The guy with the shotgun turns his wheels around and shoots your fellow officer in the face with a shotgun. What do you do? What do you do? (shoot) Who do you shoot? It's a crowded Friday afternoon, there are people everywhere. You shoot, you kill other people?

"The guy with the shotgun is now running down the street. His back is turned to you. He's running away, headed into the crowd. What do you do? What do you do? Do you chase him? Do you leave your fellow officer bleeding to death on the sidewalk? The guy's bleeding to death. Your fellow officer is dying on the sidewalk. What do you do?

"The guy with the revolver just went back into the bank. You forgot about him. He's back in the bank because you've just taken the action. He's back in the bank. He's holding a young lady teller with a revolver to her head. You go in the bank, he tells you to put down your gun. What do you do? (Call for backup) What? He's about to blow her head off! You call for back-up? What do you do? That's what you're here for. You don't put your gun down. He blows her head off.

"That scenario is over with. You're in a restaurant. You're armed, off duty, it's a Saturday afternoon. An armed robbery goes down. What do you do? You're sworn to protect people. What do you do? It's crowded, what do you do?

"OK, that scenario is over with. You're in another business. Let's say there's another robber. You don't have a gun. It goes down. What do you do? You're standing right next to the guy. What do you do? Aren't you sworn to take action? What do you do? The whole thing is over with. It's over with."

> Taking the oral board can be an incredibly stressful experience, as you can see. You'll walk out of the oral board feeling either nauseated or very proud. The goal of this book is to prepare you to feel the pride, not the nausea. The role playing practice tips that follow will help ensure this.

PREPARATION MAKES PERFECT

Many people feel uncomfortable blowing their own horn. Those who are ultimately hired find a tactful and effective way of convincing interviewers that they are the most qualified applicant. To do well during an interview or oral board you must focus the discussion on what you have to offer the agency, then seize the opportunity to impress the interviewers with the professional quality and content of your responses.

To be effective in an interview situation, you must practice, and the best way to do it is through role playing. This is not an easy task for most people because it is an unusual experience. Practice is the only way to become good at it, but people who really want a career in law enforcement will make the effort to practice and prepare themselves. They will find the time and determination to develop and fine-tune their newly acquired skill of selling themselves.

By practicing role playing, you will learn how to present the values, behaviors, and skills you possess that fit the needs of the agency. This presentation must be made with an attitude that says as clearly as words, "Hey, I'm the perfect person for the job! I know it, and I intend to prove it to you beyond the shadow of a doubt." By playing out the situation before it actually occurs, you can be sure you are projecting the image you want.

How to Practice Role Playing

There are three good ways to practice role playing: using a tape recorder, with a friend or relative, and in front of a mirror. Regardless of which method you choose, your objective is to enhance your skills by practicing, receiving feedback on how well you did, incorporating those suggestions, and then practicing again. Concentrate on evaluating the following:

1. Your body positioning
2. Your facial expressions
3. Your hand gestures
4. Your clothing and overall appearance
5. Your word selection and patterns
6. The tone and inflection of your voice.

You'll find your anxieties are greatly reduced when you reach the oral board because you will be much better prepared. Your enhanced skills will allow you to be much more in control during the interview, and your increased self-confidence and communication ability will help you convey your thoughts more clearly.

Take the list of questions and the answers you wrote from Steps 15 and 17. Practice reading these questions aloud, then answer them without reading the answers verbatim. Do this repeatedly by yourself until you find the answers for each question coming easily and naturally to you.

Next, begin using a tape recorder. Record your answers and begin to evaluate your word selection, voice qualities, and specific answers. Make sure your volume is sufficient, that your word patterns are positive and optimistic, that you use empathy and sincerity at appropriate moments, and that your answers are concise and to the point.

Progress to practicing in front of a mirror as your next step. Observe and analyze your body positioning, facial expressions, gestures, and appearance. If you have access to a videotape recorder, you can get even more helpful feedback.

Finally, perform in front of friends or relatives. Explain that the goal of your role playing practice is to create a realistic interview environment in which you can improve your skills. Find someone who will give you honest, candid, and intelligent feedback. This will help you develop a presentation that doesn't sound canned. It also helps create some of the spontaneity you need to be persuasive. Ask your assistant to read the questions out of order and with slightly different wording so that you don't become too set on one style of presentation. Above all, work hard! Evaluate, role play some more, and continue to evaluate.

While practicing, you must concentrate on creating a professional image while staying natural and saying exactly what you need to say. The more you practice, the better you will become. Your professional image will convey that you are a stable, decisive, motivated, intelligent individual. Interviewers must be convinced that you are dedicated and have good leadership skills and that you are results-oriented, mature, and ethical. Toward this end, your intelligence and quick-mindedness must be apparent.

QUESTIONS • COMMENTS • THINGS TO DO

"People with goals succeed because they know where they're going."

—**Earl Nightingale**

ORAL BOARD DOS AND DON'TS
AND SEND TEN COVER LETTERS/RESUMES

DATE:

OBJECTIVE:

To learn the basic actions and behaviors that will get you through your oral board without incident and to send ten cover letters and resumes.

PURPOSE:

As we discussed in the section on interview techniques, there is much more to an interview than just being able to answer the interviewer's questions. You must also be able to leave the interviewer(s) with an overall positive impression of you.

Today's assignments will teach you specific strategies for playing—and winning—the oral board game. Learn these techniques well and use them. Remember, making a good impression on your interviewers is just as important as your qualifications; the little extra touches you add in an interview situation are what make you stand out from the others.

By sending out ten cover letters and resumes, you've completed the process of contacting an initial thirty agencies. But don't stop there! Now that you've got the procedure down, continue on your own and keep contacting new agencies on a regular basis.

TIME REQUIRED: Three hours.

ASSIGNMENTS:

1. Study the section titled "A Few Days Before Your Oral Board."
2. Study the section titled "Immediately Prior to Your Oral Board."
3. Study the section titled "During Your Oral Board."
4. Study the checklist, "A Few Don'ts."
5. Send out ten cover letters and resumes.

A Few Days Before Your Oral Board

1. Confirm the exact date, time, place, interviewer's full name and title, and purpose of the interview.
2. Assemble extra copies of your resume and references in case you need to speak to more than one person.
3. Review a copy of your application. Be prepared to answer questions about what you have written. The department has done a thorough check on you before the interview. If you have any kind of a record, criminal or otherwise, they know about it. They may also have chatted with your neighbors or former employers. Be prepared to answer questions about any incidents the interviewers may have discovered in their background check.
4. Do research on the department for which you are being interviewed. Read the exam bulletin, job specification, and any other applicable material and talk to several people already in that job classification to find out what they do.
5. Make lists of questions you would like to ask about this opening, as well as questions you may be asked; this was discussed in steps 15 and 17.
6. Role-play answering questions you think you may be asked.
7. Make sure you know how to get to the interview and plan your route and transportation. If you are unfamiliar with the location of the interview you might want to do a trial run. If you are traveling a long distance to the interview, carefully work out the details to allow plenty of time for travel difficulties.
8. Make personal arrangements, such as taking time off from your current job, arranging childcare, and so forth.

Immediately Prior to Your Oral Board

1. Be good to yourself the day of the interview. If you feel good you will portray a positive image. Do not go out carousing the

night before—get plenty of sleep. If you are particularly nervous, go to a movie or take a long walk to help you relax and get your mind off the interview. Eat a nutritious meal before you head off to the interview.

2. Think positive thoughts; visualize yourself carrying off the interview successfully.

3. Always come well dressed! It is important to be neat, clean, and well-groomed at your interview. The panel may try to visualize you in uniform; if they see a sloppy applicant, they will also see a sloppy uniformed officer. This will be a black mark against you immediately.

   In addition to dressing well, dress conservatively. Men should wear a conservative suit with a jacket and tie. Make sure your clothes are neat, clean, pressed, free of lint, and color-coordinated. Your tie should be straight and tied properly. Shine your shoes and wear dress socks, not sweat socks. Make sure your nails are clipped and your hands are clean. Your hair must be cut short (at least above your collar and around your ears) and neatly combed. Be clean-shaven; shave off your sideburns, beard, and mustache before the interview. You can always grow them back later if the department permits it. Women should wear a conservative skirt and jacket. Make sure whatever you wear is neat and clean and stick to "earth tones." Don't wear anything too bright, or excessively feminine or sexy. Your skirt should come at least to your knee, and you should wear flat or low-heeled pumps. Double-check your stockings for runs and snags and make sure your slip does not show. Make-up should be light and look natural, not dramatic. Wear clear nail polish or none at all and clip your nails short. If your hair is long, tie it back or put it in a bun. Wear small gold or silver earrings, nothing bright or dangling. You may wish to wear a watch and/or wedding ring and a simple chain around your neck, but no more. Never wear excessive jewelry or perfume.

4. Try to overcome nervousness by taking a deep breath, but don't worry if you can't shake the feeling completely. "Nervousness on the part of the applicant is expected," said one police chief. "We would think there was something wrong with someone who wasn't a little unnerved when walking into a room with six uniformed policemen sitting there in a row. Nervousness is not a black mark against the candidate."

DURING YOUR ORAL BOARD

1. On your arrival, ask to use the restroom, hang up your coat, and so forth, if necessary. Don't wait until you're in the interview.

2. Be pleasant and courteous to everyone you meet. Everyone counts.

3. Read any agency literature or other literature in the waiting area. The magazines and brochures you find will give you clues about the interests of the people in this agency. Look around you, observing the people and decor. This will help you adjust to the environment.

4. When you first meet the interviewers, say, "It's nice to meet you." If anyone offers to shake your hand, either at the beginning or the end of the interview, shake firmly, but do not pump. A good, firm handshake shows strength and self-confidence.

5. Act as though you are looking forward to the interview. Portray your interest in the job; your enthusiasm will be noticed with approval.

6. Wait until you are offered a chair before you sit down. Once seated, sit up straight in your seat. Men may cross their legs; women should cross their ankles and sit with their legs together and to one side. Both men and women should sit with their hands folded neatly in their laps.

7. Avoid smoking, chewing gum, eating, or drinking, even if they are offered.

8. Make frequent eye contact with the interviewers. Looking directly at another person when speaking is an effective way to communicate sincerity. If you cannot look the interviewers in the eye, look at the bridge of the nose; they will think you are making eye contact. Direct most of your attention to the person in charge, but don't neglect the other interviewers. Focus most of your attention on the person who asks the question.

9. Always be polite and courteous; be straightforward, businesslike, and proper. Always answer questions with "Yes sir" and "No sir." Do not act overly friendly, crack jokes, or smile too much; the interviewers may think you're insincere or wonder what's so funny.

10. Avoid acting either too passive or too aggressive—either extreme is undesirable. A police officer must be assertive, and

hesitancy or timidity will be a mark against you. On the other hand, overly assertive or aggressive candidates may be viewed as too risky. They may create discipline problems as employees, or they may overreact in a stressful situation on the street.

11. Answer all questions succinctly and as accurately as possible. Do not ramble or become redundant. Also, do not rush to answer a difficult question. Take a few seconds to reflect and organize your thoughts, if necessary.

12. Speak in an educated and articulate manner. Speak clearly and slowly; enunciate your words so you will be understood. Do not mumble or talk to the floor. Good communication skills are important.

13. Do not give short "yes" or "no" answers. You are trying to tell the interviewers as much as possible about yourself. Give concrete, specific examples to support your answers whenever possible rather than stopping at a simple "yes" or "no." It will make your conversation more interesting and will save the interviewers the trouble of constantly asking you to elaborate or be more specific.

14. Highlight your good qualities; if you're asked about your worst quality, turn it into a positive (discussed earlier).

15. Never complain about the system or yourself. You don't want the panel to think you are a negative person or a whiner. Be enthusiastic about your past and your future.

16. Be prepared to talk about all aspects of your past, even if the information is on your application. If you are older than 25 or so, you will probably encounter a question like, "What have you been doing for the past 10 years?"

17. If you are in exceedingly good health and physical condition, bring it up as an important contribution to the department. It will be an asset to your job and the interviewers should know about it.

18. Prove you can handle yourself in tense situations. The panel will be trying to fluster you and may throw you a few curves. Think through your answers and then carefully answer the question; never rush with any answer. The panel will not mind if you pause before answering questions; they will merely see you as intelligent and thoughtful.

A Few Don'ts

Don't be late. If you are a consistently late person, plan to arrive 20 minutes early and walk around the block until the exact time you are scheduled to arrive at the interview.

Don't park in a space designated for a company employee.

Don't lie or evade questions.

Don't offer references unless asked. You should, however, bring the reference list in case you are asked for one.

Don't interrupt. Your interviewers may feel you are being rude or acting in a manner inappropriate for an applicant.

Don't criticize previous employers, companies, or employees. You can only hurt yourself, not them.

Don't patronize the interviewer for any reason. Interviewers sometimes make statements in an inconsiderate manner to see if you become irritated.

Don't stare blankly at the interviewer when you are listening. Always be alert.

Don't end the interview before you are dismissed.

Don't continue to talk after the interviewer has concluded the interview.

Send Ten Cover Letters and Resumes

Record below the names of the agencies you contact.

1. _____
2. _____
3. _____
4. _____
5. _____
6. _____
7. _____
8. _____
9. _____
10. _____

STEP 20

"All of the significant battles are waged within the self."

—Sheldon Kopp

FEDERAL LAW ENFORCEMENT POSITIONS

DATE:

OBJECTIVE:

To become aware of law enforcement positions available within the federal government and their respective employment procedures and requirements.

PURPOSE:

When considering a professional career in law enforcement, you should not overlook a key employer—the U.S. government. Remember, the more positions you apply for, the more likely you are to get the job you're after! This section will give you a brief overview of some of the options available to you in government employment.

TIME REQUIRED: Three hours.

ASSIGNMENT:

Read and understand the section titled "Finding Federal Jobs." Then go through the application process for any of the jobs you find interesting.

FINDING FEDERAL JOBS

Most federal civilian jobs are classified as "competitive service" and are filed through the Office of Personnel Management (OPM). When government hiring officials have vacancies, they notify OPM and request the names of qualified candidates from an Eligibility List. In essence, the OPM acts as a national clearinghouse of applicants.

Your main source will be the Federal Job Information Centers, which are maintained by the OPM. To find the closest one to you, look under U.S. Government in your local phone directory or contact

Federal Jobs Information Office
Office of Personnel Management
1900 'E' Street NW
Washington, DC 20415
phone (202) 606-2700.

Your local State Employment Security Office also receives and posts federal job announcements.

Some agencies do not use the OPM; they hire directly instead. These agencies include the Central Intelligence Agency, the Federal Bureau of Investigation and the Foreign Service of the Department of State. In these "excepted service" cases, you should contact the hiring agency directly.

When contacting any job source, be prepared; know the specific position or type of position you are seeking and the geographic areas in which you are willing to work. Your chances of being hired will depend on how fast vacancies are occurring in the areas in which you would like to work, the number of qualified persons who have applied for the position, and the minimum salary you will accept.

Always read the job announcement carefully; make sure you qualify for the position. It's easy to waste valuable time and effort applying for positions either in areas where you are not willing to work or for which you are not qualified. Pay particular attention to the physical requirements of age and vision.

Filing the Application

The majority of federal civilian jobs require you to file an application called the SF-171. You can obtain this form at a Federal Jobs Information Center or request that one be sent to you from the OPM.

Fill out the SF-171 completely and thoroughly; this is the form from which you will be rated and evaluated. List all your education, training, work experience, certificates, and volunteer experiences. This information will be the basis for your GS rating, which is used by the government in determining your job class.

You will probably be required to take a written examination as well. If you pass, your name will go on a list of qualified applicants. It is then referred to agencies for job consideration in order of your standing on the list and in accordance with veteran's preference laws. Your name remains on the list until you are hired or until the eligibility list expires.

FEDERAL GOVERNMENT JOB OPPORTUNITIES

1. Border Patrol Agent

The Border Patrol is a division of the Immigration and Naturalization Service (INS). The Border Patrol's primary responsibilities are to detect and prevent the illegal entry or smuggling of aliens into the United States and to detect, take into custody, and arrange for the deportation of those living illegally in this country. Border patrol agents perform their work along more than 8,000 miles of U.S. international boundaries.

Candidates must be between the ages of 21 and 35 at the time of appointment. High school graduates (or those with a G.E.D.) are preferred. A passing grade on a written OPM entrance exam and a qualifying rating from a panel of interviewers are also required. Knowledge of Spanish is a plus. A complete medical exam will be given to all applicants to determine physical and mental fitness. There are vision requirements; ask when applying. A thorough background investigation is conducted to determine character, honesty, and general suitability. All candidates must have a valid driver's license.

Newly hired border patrol agents undergo sixteen weeks of training at the Border Patrol Academy in Glynco, Georgia. After graduation, trainees return to their original duty stations and begin work. New agents receive a career-conditional appointment that leads to a permanent career appointment after three years of continuous and satisfactory service.

Candidates for Border Patrol Agent positions are selected from the OPM register of persons meeting the basic entrance requirements. Once hired, the prospects for advancement are excellent.

2. Customs Inspector

Customs Inspectors help enforce U.S. customs regulations through examination, inspection, and questioning. Their responsibilities include cargo and baggage; articles worn or carried by individuals; and vessels, vehicles, and aircraft entering or leaving the United States. They are also responsible for examining crew and passenger lists, health clearances, stores lists, ships' documents, and issuing required permits. If wrongdoing is suspected, they may conduct body searches of crew members to check for contraband.

Candidates for the position of Customs Inspector must be U.S. citizens at least 21 years of age with a high school education. Other requirements include three years of paid experience in government, business, or the armed forces in positions that involved dealing with the public, applying regulations, or using instructional materials. A qualifying score on the Professional and Administrative Career Examination (PACE) and successful completion of an oral interview are also needed. Each candidate will go through a medical examination to determine physical and mental stability. All candidates must also pass a thorough background investigation.

New hires receive extensive on-the-job and classroom training. After completion of a probationary period, usually one year, the trainee receives permanent employment status.

Customs Inspector positions are obtained through the competitive civil service system of the federal government. If you are a current or former federal employee, contact

> U.S. Customs Service
> Office of Human Resources
> Enforcement Division
> P.O. Box 7108
> Washington, DC 20044

3. Deputy U.S. Marshal

Under the direction of the 94 U.S. Marshals, Deputy U.S. Marshals perform a variety of law enforcement duties. Deputies have primary responsibility for providing security to the federal courts; insuring the personal safety of judges, jurors, and attorneys; and looking after the physical security of court buildings and facilities. Deputies also perform investigative duties in the execution of arrest warrants for federal probation, parole, mandatory release, and bond default violators and in the apprehension of federal escapees. They maintain custody of federal prisoners from the time of arrest to their sentencing or release, and transport federal prisoners between court and prison facilities. They may also perform specialized law enforcement functions for the U.S. Attorney General.

Candidates for these positions must be U.S. citizens between the ages of 21 and 35 at the time of appointment, with at least three years of general work experience in one of a wide range of areas; ask for details. Candidates must also qualify on a written OPM examination and go through an interview to be placed on an eligibility list. A personal background investigation is conducted. Each candidate must have a valid driver's license.

Newly hired deputies enter a twelve-week basic training program at the Federal Law Enforcement Training Center (FLETC) in Glynco, Georgia. After completing the program, new deputies work with experienced personnel until they have enough experience to work independently.

Candidates for the position of Deputy U.S. Marshal are selected from an eligibility list. Competition among candidates is keen, but, once hired, the applicant's opportunity for advancement is generally good.

4. Officer, U.S. Secret Service Uniformed Division

The Secret Service Uniformed Division is composed of two main sections, the White House and the Foreign Missions branches. Officers of the White House branch protect the president and family members, guard the White House complex, and safeguard other locations housing presidential offices. Foreign Missions officers provide protection and security for foreign diplomatic missions in any area as ordered by the President. In addition, Uniformed Division officers help protect the vice president, family members, and official residence.

Uniformed Division officers are authorized to enforce all laws related to their protective responsibilities and are expected to employ sound, professional law enforcement practices. They are fully trained for all types of assignments and are ready to respond to a variety of situations, from routine patrol to handling bomb threats to arresting individuals breaking laws within Uniformed Service jurisdiction.

Candidates for the Uniformed Division, as with any division of the Secret Service, are carefully selected. They must be U.S. citizens at least

21 years of age with a high school diploma or equivalent, or work experience as a police officer. They must pass a written exam and qualify on a personal interview. A medical exam is given to determine physical and mental fitness. A comprehensive background check is made on each qualifying candidate. Candidates must be able to work rotating shifts, including weekends, and possess a valid driver's license.

Newly hired officers are given extensive training at federal law enforcement training centers in Beltsville, Maryland, and Brunswick, Georgia. Classroom instruction is supplemented by on-the-job training. New officers are assigned on a probationary basis. Permanent appointments are made after successful completion of the probationary period.

Candidates are selected from an eligibility list. Competition is stiff because of the large number of applicants and the low rate of turnover within this division. Once hired, the Uniformed Division offers favorable career-development prospects, and provides opportunities for participation in advanced in-service training programs.

5. Special Agent, Bureau of Alcohol, Tobacco, and Firearms

ATF Special Agents have two major areas of responsibility. First, they enforce federal laws regarding the sale, transfer, manufacture, import, and possession of firearms and explosives. Second, they are responsible for enforcing federal liquor and tobacco regulations.

ATF Special Agents, working alone or in teams, gather data and plan the conduct of the investigation. They interview, observe, and interrogate suspects, informants, and witnesses. They engage in surveillance activities. They may also engage in undercover work and may conduct raids on suspected locations.

Candidates must be U.S. citizens between the ages of 21 and 35 at the time of appointment, and must hold a bachelor's degree from an accredited college or university. Certain work experience may be substituted for a college degree. Candidates must qualify on the Treasury Enforcement Agent Examination, administered by the OPM, and on a personal interview. A qualifying medical examination determines the candidate's mental and physical fitness for the position. Finally, a comprehensive background check is made on each applicant.

Newly hired agents go through an intensive training and development program that combines eight weeks of study at the Federal Law Enforcement Training Center in Georgia with closely supervised on-the-job training. After successfully completing training, new agents are assigned to BATF field offices where they work under the guidance of experienced ATF Special Agents.

Candidates are selected from an eligibility list. Competition is stiff, but, once hired, prospects for upward mobility are favorable. Agents who demonstrate the ability to assume more difficult and responsible assignments are recommended for promotion by supervisory personnel. For additional information on employment as a Special Agent, write to

Bureau of Alcohol, Tobacco and Firearms
Personnel Division
1200 Pennsylvania Ave., NW
Washington, DC 20226

6. Special Agent, Drug Enforcement Administration

DEA Special Agents primarily enforce laws dealing with narcotics and dangerous drugs by investigating the activities of major drug traffickers, both nationally and internationally. Their efforts are concentrated on locating and eliminating illegal sources of supply and distribution. Very often, hard facts and evidence about activities of illegal drug dealers cannot be obtained by conventional methods. DEA Special Agents must undertake the extremely risky work of going undercover and associating with some of society's most undesirable elements. Surveillance is also an important part of a DEA Special Agent's job, as is the regulation of legal trade in narcotic and dangerous drugs.

Candidates must be U.S. citizens between the ages of 21 and 34 at the time of appointment. Candidates must have a bachelor's degree plus one year of graduate work, an LL.B., or four years of strong work experience in a related field. A qualifying score must be obtained on the Professional and Administrative Career Examination (PACE), administered by the OPM, after which the candidate is placed on an eligibility list. Those selected from the list are given a qualifying medical examination to determine physical and mental fitness. Vision requirements apply. Each candidate is further evaluated through personal interviews, and a thorough background check is done on each candidate. A valid driver's license is required.

Newly hired agents go through a ten-week training program in Washington, DC. After concluding the training program, new agents are assigned to DEA field offices, where they work with experienced personnel until they are ready to function independently. Candidates are selected from an eligibility list. Competition for vacancies is keen; the DEA has an extremely low turnover rate. However, once hired, prospects for upward mobility are generally good. Promotions are not automatic, but based on job performance.

See the listing of who to contact for DEA jobs.

Who to Contact for DEA Jobs

Additional information may be obtained by contacting a Headquarters Personnel Office or one of the following DEA divisions.

DEA Headquarters
Washington, DC 20537
Attn: Special Agent,
Recruiting Unit

Atlanta Division
75 Spring Street, SW
Rm 740
Atlanta, GA 30303

Boston Division
50 Staniford St.
Suite 200
Boston, MA 02114

Chicago Division
500 Dirksen Federal Building
219 South Dearborn St.
Chicago, IL 60604

Dallas Division
316 U.S. Customs House
P.O. Box 1860
Denver, CO 80201

Detroit Division
357 Federal Building
231 W. Lafayette
Detroit, MI 48226

Houston Division
333 West Loop North
Houston, TX 77024

Los Angeles Division
350 S. Figueroa St.
Suite 800
Los Angeles, CA 90071

Miami Division
8400 NW 53rd St.
Suite 800
Miami, FL 33166

Newark Division
Federal Office Building
970 Broad St.
Suite 806
Newark, NJ 07102

New Orleans Division
1661 Canal St.
Suite 2200
New Orleans, LA 70112

Philadelphia Division
William J. Green Federal Bldg.
600 Arch Street
Room 10224
Philadelphia, PA 19106

Phoenix Division
One North First St.
Suite 201
Phoenix, AZ 85004

San Diego Division
402 W. 35th St.
National City, CA 92050

San Francisco Division
450 Golden Gate Avenue
Room 12215
P.O. Box 36035
San Francisco, CA 94102

Seattle Division
220 West Mercer St.
Suite 301
Seattle, WA 98119

St. Louis Division
United Bank Building
7911 Forsyth Blvd.
Suite 500
St. Louis, MO 63105

Washington Division
400 Sixth Street, SW
Room 2558
Washington, DC 20024

7. Special Agent, FBI

The FBI investigates more than 200 different types of cases resulting from violations of federal laws. It is a fact-gathering agency whose Special Agents function as investigators. It does not prosecute cases, but turns over facts and evidence to a U.S. attorney. FBI Special Agents are responsible for enforcing a wide variety of federal laws within their jurisdiction, dealing with such matters as kidnapping, bank robbery, theft of government property, organized crime activity, espionage, sabotage, civil rights violations, and white-collar crimes such as bank embezzlements or bankruptcy fraud. Under certain circumstances, agents may work undercover to observe suspects and gather evidence needed to build or solve a case. Surveillance activity is also an important part of an FBI Special Agent's work. Most FBI agents are assigned to one of the 59 divisional offices located in cities throughout the United States and Puerto Rico.

Candidates must be U.S. citizens between the ages of 23 and 34 and must be willing to be assigned to work anywhere within the United States or Puerto Rico. There are five entrance programs under which applicants can qualify for possible appointment: law, accounting, language, modified, and science. Different requirements apply for each. All candidates must qualify on a battery of written and oral examinations designed to measure personality characteristics. Each candidate must pass a difficult physical examination; be capable of strenuous physical exertion; and have excellent hearing, eyesight, and color vision. An extensive background check is conducted on all applicants.

Newly hired agents undergo fifteen weeks of training at the FBI Academy in Quantico, Virginia. After completing training, new agents are appointed on a probationary basis and team with experienced agents. After one year of satisfactory performance, they receive permanent employment status.

The turnover rate for Special Agents in the FBI is very low, and it is difficult to obtain positions. Once in the agency, supervisory and administrative positions are filled by agents from within the organization, and promotions are based on demonstrated leadership qualities and work experience.

QUESTIONS • COMMENTS • THINGS TO DO

APPENDIX

BENEFICIAL FACTS AND RESOURCES

FEDERAL LAW ENFORCEMENT AGENCIES

Bureau of Alcohol, Tobacco and Firearms
650 Massachusetts Ave., NW
Washington, DC 20226
(202) 927-8700   Fax (202) 927-8876

Federal Bureau of Investigation
J Edgar Hoover Building
Washington, DC 20535
(202) 324-3000   Fax (202) 324-4705

Drug Enforcement Administration
Washington, DC 20537
(202) 307-8000   Fax (202) 307-7335

Financial Crime Enforcement Network
2070 Chain Bridge Rd.
Vienna, VA 22182
(703) 905-3591   Fax (703) 905-3690

National Park Service—US Park Police
Ohio Dr. SW
Washington, DC 20242
(202) 619-7350   Fax (202) 205-7981

US Customs Service
1300 Pennsylvania Ave., NW, Suite 44A
Washington, DC 20229
(202) 927-1010   Fax (202) 927-1380

US Department of Treasury
1500 Pennsylvania Ave., NW
Washington, DC 20220
(202) 622-1100   Fax (202) 622-0073

US Fish & Wildlife Service
4401 N. Fairfax Dr.
Arlington, VA 22203
(703) 358-1949   Fax (703) 358-2271

US Marshals Service
600 Army Navy Dr.
Arlington, VA 22202
(202) 307-9001   Fax (202) 557-9788

ORGANIZATIONS THAT PROVIDE LAW ENFORCEMENT TRAINING

American Society of Law Enforcement Trainers (ASLET)
P. O. Box 361
Lewes, DE 19958
(302) 645-4080   Fax (302) 645-4084

Association of Public Safety Communications Officials International Inc.
2040 S. Ridgeway Ave.
South Daytona, FL 32119
(904) 322-2500   Fax (904) 322-2501

Canada Association of Chiefs of Police (CACP)
130 Albert St., Suite 1710
Ottawa, ON K1P 5G4
(613) 233-1106   Fax (613) 233-6960

Federal Law Enforcement Training Center
Glynco, GA 31524
(912) 267-2224   Fax (912) 267-2495

Institute for Aerobics Research
12330 Preston Rd.
Dallas, TX 75230
(214) 701-8001

Institute of Police Technology & Management
12000 Alumni Dr.
Jacksonville, FL 32224
(904) 620-4786   Fax (904) 620-2453

International Association of Arson Investigators
25 Newton Street
P. O. Box 600
Marlboro, MA 01752
(502) 491-7482

International Association of Bomb Technicians and Investigators
P. O. Box 6609
Colorado Springs, CO 80934
(719) 636-2596

International Association of Chiefs of Police (IACP)
515 N. Washington St.
Alexandria, VA 22314
(800) 843-4227   Fax (703) 836-4543

International Association of Ethics Trainers
10600 West SR 434, Suite 164
Longwood, FL 32750
(407) 339-0322   Fax (407) 339-7139

International Association of Financial Crimes Investigators
385 Belmarin Keys Blvd., Suite H
Novato, CA 94949
(415) 884-6600   Fax (415) 884-6605

International Association of Fire Chiefs
4025 Fair Ridge Rd.
Fairfax, VA 22033
(703) 273-0911   Fax (703) 273-9363

International Association of Women Police
P. O. Box 15207
Seattle, WA 98115
(206) 625-4465

International Narcotic Enforcement Officers Association Inc.
112 State St., Suite 1200
Albany, NY 12207
(518) 253-2874   Fax (518) 253-3378

National Association of School Resource Officers
2714 SW 5th St.
Boynton Beach, FL 33435
(561) 736-1736   Fax (561) 736-1736

National Institute of Ethics
1060 West SR 434, Suite 164
Longwood, FL 32750
(407) 339-0322   Fax (407) 339-7139

National Institute on Economic Crime
P. O. Box 7186
Fairfax, VA 22039
(703) 250-8706   Fax (703) 860-8449

National Institute of Justice Resources
Office of the Director
810 7th St., NW
Washington, DC 20531
(202) 307-2942   Fax (202) 307-6394

National Criminal Justice Reference Service
Office of the Director
P. O. Box 6000
Rockville, MD 20849
(800) 519-5500   Fax (301) 519-5212

Bureau of Justice Assistance Clearinghouse
(800) 688-4252   Fax (410) 953-3848

Juvenile Justice Clearinghouse
(800) 638-8736   Fax (301) 519-5212

National Victims Resource Center
(800) 627-6872   Fax (410) 953-3848

LAW ENFORCEMENT RELATED ASSOCIATIONS

AAA Foundation for Traffic Safety
1440 New York Ave. NW #201
Washington, DC 20005
(202) 638-5944   Fax (202) 638-5943

Air Force Security Police Association
818 Willow Creek Cir.
San Marcos, TX 78666-5060
(800) 782-7653   Fax (512) 396-7328

Air Incident Research
P.O. Box 4745
East Lansing, MI 48826
(517) 336-9375   Fax (517) 336-9375

Airborne Law Enforcement Association Inc.
14268 Linda Vista Dr.
Whittier, CA 90602
(213) 485-2011   Fax (213) 485-2073

American Association of Retired Persons (AARP)
601 E St. NW
Washington, DC 20049
(202) 434-2222   Fax (202) 434-6466

American Association of State Highway and Transportation Officials
444 N. Capitol St. NW, Suite 249
Washington, DC 20001
(202) 434-2222   Fax (202) 434-6466

American Correctional Association
4380 Forbes Blvd.
Lanham, MD 20706
(301) 918-1800   Fax (301) 918-1900

American Criminal Justice Association
P. O. Box 601047
Sacramento, CA 95860
(916) 484-6553   Fax (916) 488-2227

American Federation of Police and Concerned Citizens
3801 Biscayne Blvd.
Miami, FL 33137
(305) 573-0070   Fax (305) 573-9819

American Jail Association
2053 Day Rd., Suite 100
Hagerstown, MD 21740
(301) 790-3930   Fax (301) 790-2941

American Planning Association
1776 Massachusetts Ave., NW, Suite 400
Washington, DC 20036
(202) 872-0611   Fax (202) 872-0643

American Police Hall of Fame and Museum
3801 Biscayne Blvd.
Miami, FL 33137
(305) 573-0070   Fax (305) 573-9819

American Police Officers Association
2173 Embassy Dr.
Lancaster, PA 17603
(888) 644-8022

American Polygraph Association
P. O. Box 8037
Chattanooga, TN 37414
(423) 892-3992   Fax (423) 894-5435

American Probation & Parole Association
2760 Research Park Dr.
Lexington, KY 40578
(606) 244-3216   Fax (606) 244-8001

American Psychiatric Association
1400 K St., NW
Washington, DC 20005
(202) 682-6000   Fax (202) 682-6850

American Society of Law Enforcement Trainers (ASLET)
P. O. Box 361
Lewes, DE 19958
(302) 645-4080   Fax (302) 645-4084

Americans for Effective Law Enforcement Inc.
5519 W. Cumberland Ave., #1008
Chicago, IL 60656
(800) 763-2802   Fax (800) 763-3221

Association of American Railroads
P. O. Box 11130
Pueblo, CO 81001
(719) 584-0701   Fax (719) 585-1819

Association of Public Safety Communications Officials International Inc.
2040 S. Ridgeway Ave.
South Daytona, FL 32119
(904) 322-2500   Fax (904) 322-2501

Blacks in Law Enforcement Inc.
156 E. McLemore Ave.
Memphis, TN 38106
(901) 774-1118   Fax (901) 774-1139

Canada Association of Chiefs of Police (CACP)
130 Albert St., Suite 1710
Ottawa, ON K1P 5G4
(613) 233-1106   Fax (613) 233-6960

Child Find of America, Inc.
P. O. Box 277
New Paltz, NY 12561
(914) 255-1848   Fax (914) 255-5706

Child Shield USA
103 W. Spring St.
Titusville, PA 16354
(800) 652-4453   Fax (814) 827-6977

Commission on Accreditation For Law Enforcement
10306 Eaton Pl., Suite 320
Fairfax, VA 22030
(800) 368-3757   Fax (703) 591-2206

Concerns of Police Survivors Inc.
South Highway 5
Camdenton, MO 65020
(573) 346-4911   Fax (573) 346-1414

Congressional Fire Services Institute
900 Second St., NE Suite 303
Washington, DC 20002
(202) 371-1277   Fax (202) 682-3473

Council of International Investigators
27999 Clemmons Rd.
Cleveland, OH 44145
(440) 892-1000   Fax (440) 892-9439

Crime Stoppers International
P. O. Box 30413
Albuquerque, NM 87190
(817) 446-6253   Fax (817) 446-6253

D-A-R-E- America
P. O. Box 512090
Los Angeles, CA 90051
(310) 215-0575   Fax (310) 215-0180

Eastern Armed Robbery Conference LTD
P. O. Box 5772
Wilmington, DE 19808
(516) 852-6271   Fax (516) 852-6478

Federal Law Enforcement Officers Association
P. O. Box 508
East Northport, NY 11731
(516) 368-6117   Fax (516) 368-6429

Federal Pretrial Services Agency
500 Pearl St., Rm 550
New York, NY 10007
(212) 805-0015   Fax (212) 805-4172

Hostage Negotiators of America
2072 Edinburgh Dr.
Montgomery, AL 36116
(334) 244-7411

Institute of Police Technology & Management
12000 Alumni Dr.
Jacksonville, FL 32224
(904) 620-4786   Fax (904) 620-2453

International Association of Ethics Trainers
1060 West SR 434, Suite 164
Longwood, FL 32750
(407) 339-0322   Fax (407) 339-7139

International Association for Identification
2535 Pilot Knob Rd., Suite 117
Mendota Heights, MN 55120
(651) 681-8566   Fax (651) 681-8443

International Association for Property and Evidence
904 N. San Fernando Blvd., Suite 4
Burbank, CA 91504
(800) 449-4273   Fax (818) 846-4543

International Association of Bomb Technicians and Investigators
P. O. Box 8629
Naples, FL 34101
(941) 353-6843   Fax (941) 353-6841

International Association of Campus Law Enforcement Administrators (IACP)
342 N. Main St.
West Hartford, CT 06117
(860) 586-7517   Fax (860) 586-7550

International Association of Chiefs of Police (IACP)
515 N. Washington St.
Alexandria, VA 22314
(800) 843-4227   Fax (703) 836-4543

International Association of Correctional Officers
3900 Industrial Ave.
Lincoln, NE 68504
(402) 464-0602   Fax (402) 464-5931

International Association of Financial Crimes Investigators
385 Belmarin Keys Blvd., Suite H
Novato, CA 94949
(415) 884-6600   Fax (415) 884-6605

International Association of Fire Chiefs
4025 Fair Ridge Rd.
Fairfax, VA 22033
(703) 273-0911   Fax (703) 273-9363

International Association of Law Enforcement Planners
1000 Connecticut Ave., Suite 9
Washington, DC 20036
(202) 857-8485

International Association of Personal Protection Agents
458 W. Kenwood
Brighton, TN 38011
(901) 837-1915   Fax (901) 837-4949

International Association of Women Police
5413 W. Sunnyside Ave.
Chicago, IL 60630
(773) 736-3405

International City/County Management Association (ICMA)
777 N. Capitol St. NE, Suite 500
Washington, DC 20002
(202) 289-4262   Fax (202) 962-3500

International Conference of Police Chaplains
P. O. Box 5590
Destin, FL 32540
(850) 654-9736   Fax (850) 654-9742

International Fire Marshals Association
1 Batterymarch Park
Quincy, MA 02269
(617) 984-7424   Fax (617) 984-7056

International Foundation for Art Research
500 5th Ave., Suite 1234
New York, NY 10101
(212) 391-6234   Fax (212) 391-8794

International Foundation for Protection Officers
3106 Tami Annie Trail
Naples, FL 34103
(941) 430-0534   Fax (941) 430-5333

International Juvenile Officers Association Inc.
P. O. Box 56
Easton, CT 06612
(203) 377-4424

International Law Enforcement Stress Association
5485 David Blvd.
Port Charlotte, FL 33981
(813) 697-8863

International Narcotic Enforcement Officers Association Inc.
112 State St., Suite 1200
Albany, NY 12207
(518) 253-2874   Fax (518) 253-3378

International Police Association—US Section
P. O. Box 43-1822
Miami, FL 33243
(305) 253-2874   Fax (305) 253-3568

International Police Mountain Bike Association
28 E. Ostend St.
Baltimore, MD 21230
(410) 685-2220   Fax (410) 685-2240

International Prisoners Aid Association
Dept. of Sociology, University of Louisville
Louisville, KY 40292
(502) 241-7831   Fax (502) 241-7831

International Union of Police Association AFL/CIO
1421 Prince St., Suite 330
Alexandria, VA 22314
(703) 549-7434   Fax (703) 549-9048

Jewelers Security Alliance
6 E. 45th St.
New York, NY 10017
(800) 537-0067   Fax (212) 808-9168

Law Enforcement Alliance of America
7700 Leesburg Pike, Suite 421
Falls Church, VA 22043
(703) 847-2677   Fax (703) 556-6485

Law Enforcement and Emergency Services Video Association
P. O. Box 126167
Fort Worth, TX 76126
(817) 249-4002   Fax (817) 249-4002

Law Enforcement Memorial Association Inc.
P.O. Box 72835
Roselle, IL 60172
(847) 795-1547   Fax (847) 795-2469

Military Police Regimental Association
P. O. Box 5278
Anniston, AL 36205
(256) 848-5014   Fax (256) 848-6691

Missing Children Society of Canada
3501 23rd St., NE, Suite 219
Calgary, AB T2E 6V8
(403) 291-0705   Fax (403) 291-9728

Narcotic Enforcement Officers Association
29 N. Plains Highway Phoenix Park, Suite 10
Wallingford, CT 06492
(203) 269-8940   Fax (203) 284-9103

National Association Against Gang and Domestic Violence
P. O. Box 775186
St. Louis, MO 63177
(314) 631-3723

National Association of Chiefs of Police
3801 Biscayne Blvd.
Miami, FL 33137
(305) 573-0070   Fax (305) 573-9819

National Association of Counties
440 First St. NW, 8th Floor
Washington, DC 20001
(202) 393-6226   Fax (202) 393-2630

National Association of Drug Court Professionals
901 N. Pitt St., Suite 370
Alexandria, VA 22314
(703) 706-0576   Fax (703) 706-0577

National Association of Field Training Officers (NAFTO)
Sage Valley Rd.
Longmont, CO 80503
(303) 442-0482   Fax (303) 546-6791

National Association of Medical Examiners
1402 S. Grand Blvd.
St. Louis, MO 63104
(314) 577-8298

National Association of Police Athletic Leagues
618 N. US Highway 1, Suite 201
N. Palm Beach, FL 33408
(561) 844-1823   Fax (561) 863-6120

National Association of Police Organizations (NAPO)
750 First St., Suite 920
Washington, DC 20002
(202) 842-4420   Fax (202) 842-4396

National Association of School Resource Officers
2714 SW 5th St.
Boynton Beach, FL 33435
(561) 736-1736   Fax (561) 736-1736

National Association of Town Watch
1 Wynnewood Rd., Suite 102
Wynnewood, PA 19096
(610) 649-7055   Fax (610) 649-5456

National Center for Missing and Exploited Children
2101 Wilson Blvd., Suite 550
Arlington, VA 22201
(703) 235-3900   Fax (703) 235-4067

National Child Safety Council
P. O. Box 1368
Jackson, MS 49204
(517) 764-6070   Fax (517) 764-4140

National Constable Association
16 Stonybrook Dr.
Levittown, PA 19055
(215) 547-6400   Fax (215) 943-0907

National Council on Crime and Delinquency
685 Market St., #620
San Francisco, CA 94105
(415) 896-6223   Fax (415) 896-5109

National Crime Prevention Council
1700 K St., 2nd Floor
Washington, DC 20006
(202) 466-6272   Fax (202) 296-1356

National Crime and Punishment Learning Center
623 Sarazen Dr.
Gulfport, MS 39507
(228) 896-5280   Fax (228) 896-8696

National Criminal Justice Association
444 N. Capitol St., NW, Suite 618
Washington, DC 20001
(202) 624-1440   Fax (202) 508-3859

National District Attorney's Association
99 Canal Center Plaza, Suite 510
Alexandria, VA 22314
(703) 549-9222   Fax (703) 836-3195

National Family Legal Foundation
11000 N. Scottsdale Rd., Suite 144
Scottsdale, AZ 85254
(602) 922-9731   Fax (602) 922-7240

National Fire Protection Association
1 Batterymarch Park
Quincy, MA 02269
(617) 770-3000   Fax (617) 770-0700

National Fraternal Order of Police
1410 Donelson Pike, #A17
Nashville, TN 37217
(615) 339-0900   Fax (615) 339-0400

National Institute of Ethics
1060 West SR 434, Suite 164
Longwood, FL 32750
(407) 339-0322   Fax (407) 339-7139

National Institute on Economic Crime
P. O. Box 7186
Fairfax, VA 22039
(703) 250-8706   Fax (703) 860-8449

National Insurance Crime Bureau
10330 S. Roberts Rd.
Palos Hills, IL 60465
(708) 430-2430   Fax (708) 430-2446

National Law Enforcement Council
888 16th St., NW, Suite 700
Washington, DC 20006
(202) 835-8020   Fax (202) 331-4291

National Law Enforcement Officers Memorial Fund Inc.
605 E St., NW
Washington, DC 20004
(202) 737-3400   Fax (202) 737-3405

National Law Enforcement Research Center
P. O. Box 70966
Sunnydale, CA 94086
(408) 245-2037   Fax (408) 245-2037

National League of Cities
1301 Pennsylvania Ave. NW, Suite 550
Washington, DC 20004
(202) 626-3000   Fax (202) 626-3043

National Legal Aid and Defender Association
1625 K St. NW, Suite 800
Washington, DC 20006
(202) 452-0620   Fax (202) 872-1031

National Organization for Victim Assistance
1757 Park Rd. NW
Washington, DC 20010
(202) 232-6682   Fax (202) 462-2255

National Organization of Black Law Enforcement Executives
1757 Park Rd. NW
Washington, DC 20010
(703) 658-1529   Fax (703) 658-9479

National Police Institute
Central Missouri State University, 200 Main St.
Warrensburg, MO 22312
(660) 543-4091   Fax (660) 543-83306

National Recreation and Park Association
DuPage County Forest Preserve District
Glen Ellyn, IL 60138
(630) 933-7239   Fax (630) 790-1071

National Reserve Law Officers Association
P. O. Box 6505
San Antonio, TX 78209
(210) 820-0478   Fax (210) 804-2463

National Rifle Association
11250 Waples Mill Rd.
Fairfax, VA 22030
(703) 267-1000   Fax (703) 267-3989

National Safety Council
1025 Connecticut Ave. NW, Suite 1200
Washington, DC 20036
(202) 974-2480   Fax (202) 293-0032

National Sheriffs Association
1450 Duke St.
Alexandria, VA 22314
(703) 836-7827   Fax (703) 683-6541

National Tactical Officers Association
P. O. Box 529
Doylestown, PA 18901
(800) 279-9127   Fax (215) 230-7552

National Technical Investigators Association
6933 N 26th St.
Falls Church, VA 22046
(703) 237-9388   Fax (703) 241-0353

National Traffic Law Center
99 Canal Center Plaza, Suite 510
Alexandria, VA 22314
(703) 549-4253   Fax (703) 836-3195

National Troopers Coalition
Andrea Lane
La Plata, MD 20646
(410) 653-3885   Fax (410) 653-0929

National United Law Enforcement Officers Association Inc.
265 E. McLemore Ave.
Memphis, TN 38106
(901) 774-1118   Fax (901) 774-1139

National White Collar Crime Center
7401 Beausant Springs Dr.
Richmond, VA 23225
(804) 323-3563   Fax (804) 323-3566

National Wildlife Federation
8925 Leesburg Pike
Vienna, VA 22184
(703) 790-4000   Fax (703) 790-4330

National Youth Gang Center
2894 Remington Green Circle
Tallahassee, FL 32308
(850) 385-0600   Fax (850) 385-5356

**Nine Lives Associates Executive
Protection Institute**
RR 1 Box 332
Bluemont, VA 26135
(540) 955-1128   Fax (540) 955-0255

Office of International Criminal Justice
1033 W. Van Burden St.
Chicago, IL 60607
(312) 996-9595   Fax (312) 312-0458

Office of Law Enforcement Standards
National Institute of Standards & Technology
Building, Rm. 225
Gaithersburg, MD 20899
(800) 975-2757   Fax (301) 948-0978

Operation Lifesaver
1420 King St., Suite 401
Alexandria, VA 22314
(800) 537-6224   Fax (703) 519-8267

**Operation Lookout National Center for
Missing Youth**
6320 Evergreen Way #201
Everett, WA 98203
(800) 782-7335   Fax (425) 438-4411

Organized Crime Task Force
143 Grand St.
White Plains, NY 10601
(914) 422-8780   Fax (914) 422-8795

Police Chiefs Spouses-Worldwide
1521 Sixth Ave East
Menomonie, WI 54751
(715) 235-9749

Police Communication Center
215 Church Ave. SW
Roanoke, VA 24011
(540) 853-2411   Fax (540) 853-1599

Police Executive Research Forum
1120 Connecticut Ave. NW, Suite 930
Washington, DC 20036
(202) 466-7820   Fax (202) 466-7826

**Police and Fireman's Insurance
Association**
101 E 116th St.
Carmel, IN 46032
(317) 581-1913   Fax (317) 571-5946

Police Marksman Association
6000 E. Shirley Lane
Montgomery, AL 36117
(334) 271-2010   Fax (334) 279-9267

Pretrial Services Resource Center
1325 G St., NW, Suite 770
Washington, DC 20005
(202) 638-3080   Fax (202) 347-0493

**Reserve Law Officers Association of
America**
San Antonio, TX 78217
(210) 653-5754   Fax (210) 653-9655

Retired and Disabled Police of America
1900 S. Harbor City Blvd., Suite 328
Melbourne, FL 32901
(800) 395-7376   Fax (407) 779-8046

The Police Supervisors Group
1401 Johnson Ferry Rd., Suite 328-F42
Marietta, GA 30062
(770) 321-5018   Fax (770) 321-5019

Transportation Research Board
2101 Constitution Ave. NW
Washington, DC 20418
(202) 334-2936   Fax (202) 334-2003

US Conference of Mayors
1620 Eye St. NW
Washington, DC 20006
(202) 293-7330   Fax (202) 293-2352

United States Fire Administration
National Emergency Training Center
16825 S. Seton
Emmitsburg, MD 21727
(301) 447-1200   Fax (301) 447-1102

STATE TRAINING COUNCILS AND POLICE STANDARDS COMMISSIONS

Contact your state training council or police standards commission to learn about upcoming training opportunities or to ask questions about the hiring or training requirements in your state.

R. Alan Benefield, Chief
Alabama P.O.S.T.
P. O. Box 300075
Montgomery, AL 35130-0075
(334) 242-4045   Fax (334) 242-4633

Laddie Shaw, Executive Director
Alaska Police Standards Council
P. O. Box 111200
Juneau, Alaska 99811-1200
(907) 465-4378   Fax (907) 465-3263

Rod Covey, Executive Director
Arizona P.O.S.T.
P. O. Box 6638
Phoenix, AZ 85005
(602) 223-2514   Fax (602) 223-0477

Terry Bolton, Executive Director
Arkansas Law Enforcement Training Academy
P. O. Box 3106
East Camden, AR 71701
(870) 574-1810   Fax (870) 574-2706

Kenneth O'Brien, Executive Director
California P.O.S.T.
1601 Alahambra Blvd
Sacramento, CA 95816-7053
(916) 227-2802   Fax (916) 227-2801

Michael S. Williams
Colorado P.O.S.T.
1525 Sherman Avenue, 5th Floor
Denver, CO 80203
(303) 866-5692   Fax (303) 866-5671

T. William Knapp, Executive Director
Connecticut P.O.S.T.
285 Preston Avenue
Meriden, CT 06450
(203) 238-6505   Fax (203) 238-6543

Thomas P. DiNetta, Director
Delaware State Police Training
P. O. Box 430
Dover, DE 19903
(302) 739-5903   Fax (302) 739-5945

Leon Lowry, II Director
Florida Dept. of Law Enforcement
P. O. Box 1489
Tallahassee, FL 32302-1489
(904) 410-8600   Fax (904) 410-8606

Richard Darby, Executive Director
Georgia P.O.S.T.
2175 Northlake Parkway, Suite 144
Tucker, GA 30084
(770) 473-6602   Fax (770) 473-3870

Forest Broome, Major
Honolulu Police Academy
93-093 Waipahu Depot Road
Waipahu, HI 96813
(808) 677-1474   Fax (808) 677-7394

Michael N. Becar, Executive Director
Idaho Dept. of Law Enforcement
P. O. Box 700
Meridian, ID 83680-0700
(208) 884-7250   Fax (208) 884-7295

Thomas J. Jurkanin, Executive Director
Illinois Law Enforcement Training and Standards Board
Springfield, IL 72704
(217) 782-4540   Fax (217) 524-5350

Charles Burch, Executive Director
Indiana Law Enforcement Training Board
Plainfield, IN 46168-0313
(317) 839-5191   Fax (317) 839-9741

Gene Shepard, Director
Iowa Law Enforcement Academy
P. O. Box 130
Johnston, IA 50131-0130
(515) 242-5357   Fax (515) 242-5471

Ed H. Pavey, Executive Director
Kansas Law Enforcement Training Center
P. O. Box 647
Hutchinson, KS 67504-0647
(316) 662-3378   Fax (316) 662-4720

John Bizzack, Commissioner
Kentucky Dept. of Criminal Justice Training
Kit Carson Dr., Funderbach Bldg. EKU
Richmond, KY 40475
(606) 622-2302   Fax (606) 622-2740

Michael Ranatza, Executive Director
Louisiana P.O.S.T.
1885 Wooddale Blvd., Room 208
Baton Rouge, LA 70806
(225) 925-4942   Fax (225) 925-6106

Steven R. Giorgetti, Director
Maine Criminal Justice Academy
93 Silver Street
Waterville, ME 04901
(207) 877-8000   Fax (207) 877-8027

Donald Hopkins, Executive Director
Maryland Police and Correctional Training Commission
Woodstock, MD 21163
(410) 203-1000   Fax (410) 203-1010

Kevin Harrington, Executive Director
Massachusetts C. J. Training Council
411 Waverly Oaks Road
Waltham, MA 02154
(781) 727-7827   Fax (781) 642-6898

Raymond Beach, Jr. Executive Director
Commission on Law Enforcement Standards
7426 North Canal Road
Lansing, MI 48913
(517) 322-1946   Fax (517) 322-5611

Neil Melton, Executive Director
Board of Police Officers Standards and Training
St. Paul, MN 55104
(651) 643-3060   Fax (651) 643-3072

Chris Egbert
Missouri P.O.S.T.
P. O. Box 749
Jefferson City, MO 65102
(573) 526-6174   Fax (573) 571-5399

James B. Walker, Director
Mississippi P.O.S.T.
P. O. Box 23039
Jackson, MS 39225
(601) 359-7880   Fax (601) 359-7832

Jim Oberhofer, Executive Director
Montanta P.O.S.T.
303 North Roberts
Helena, MT 59620
(406) 444-3604   (406) 444-4722

Steve Lamken, Director
Nebraska Law Enforcement Training Center
3600 North Academy Road
Grand Island, NE 68801
(308) 385-6030   Fax (308) 385-6032

Richard Clark, Chief
Nevada P.O.S.T.
2101 Sneider Avenue
Carson City, NV 89701
(775) 687-3283   Fax (775) 687-4911

Earl M. Sweeney, Director
New Hampshire P.O.S.T.
17 Fan Road
Concord, NH 03301
(603) 271-2133   Fax (603) 271-1785

Wayne Fisher, Deputy Director
New Jersey Police Training Commission
25 Market St.
Trenton, NJ 08625
(609) 984-0960   Fax (609) 984-4473

Darrel G. Hart, Director
New Mexico Dept. of Public Safety Training and Recruiting Division
Santa Fe, NM 87505
(505) 827-9251   Fax (505) 827-3449

Jerry Burrell, Director
New York Bureau for Municipal Police Division of Criminal Justice
Albany, NY 12203
(518) 457-6101   Fax (518) 457-3089

David D. Cashwell, Director
North Carolina Dept of Justice Training and Standards
114 N. Edenton St.
Raleigh, NC 27609
(919) 716-6470   Fax (919) 716-6752

Mark Gilbertson, Executive Secretary
North Dakota P.O.S.T.
600 East Blvd., Dept 504
Bismark, ND 58505
(701) 328-9966   Fax (701) 328-9988

Vernon Chenevey, Executive Director
Ohio P.O.S.T.
P. O. Box 309
London, OH 43140
(614) 466-7771   Fax (614) 728-5150

Jeanie Nelson Ph.D., Director
Oklahoma Council on Law Enforcement Education and Training
Oklahoma City, OK 73136
(405) 425-2750   Fax (405) 425-2773

Dianne Middle, Director
Dept. of Public Safety Standards and Training
Monmouth, OR 97361
(503) 378-2100   Fax (503) 838-8907

Richard Mooney, Executive Director
Pennsylvania Municipal Police Officers Education and Training Commission
Hershey, PA 17033
(717) 533-5987   Fax (717) 787-1650

Steven D. Weaver, Director
RI Municipal Police Academy Community College of RI Flanagan Campus
Lincoln, RI 02865
(401) 222-3755   Fax (401) 726-5720

William "Billy" Gibson, Director
South Carolina Criminal Justice Academy South Carolina DPS
5400 Broad River Road
Columbus, SC 29210
(803) 896-7770   Fax (803) 896-8347

Kevin Thom, Director
Rol Kebach Criminal Justice Training Center
East Hwy 34, 500 East Capital
Pierre, SD 57501
(605) 773-3584   Fax (605) 773-7203

Mark Bracy, Director
Tennessee Law Enforcement Training Academy
3025 Lebanon Rd.
Donelson, TN 37214
(615) 741-4448   Fax (615) 741-3366

Jim Dozier, Executive Director
Texas Commission on Law Enforcement Officer Standards/Education
6330 US Hwy 290 E, Suite 200
Austin, TX 78723
(512) 936-7700   Fax (512) 936-7714

Sidney Groll, Executive Director
Utah P.O.S.T.
45424 South 2700 West
Salt Lake City, UT 84119
(801) 965-4369   Fax (801) 965-4619

Gary L. Bullard, Executive Director
Vermont Criminal Justice Training Council
Rural Road 2, Box 2160
Pittsford, VT 05763
(802) 483-6228   Fax (802) 483-2343

George Gotschalk, Chief
Standards & Training Dept. of Criminal Justice Services
Richmond, VA 23219
(804) 786-6348   Fax (804) 371-8981

Michael Parsons, Ph.D. Executive Director
Washington State Criminal Justice Training Council
19010 1st Ave. S.
Seattle, WA 98148
(206) 439-3740   Fax (206) 439-3752

Don Davidson, Executive Director
West Virginia Criminal Justice and Highway Safety
1204 Kanawha Blvd., E.
Charleston, WV 25301
(304) 558-8814   Fax (304) 558-0391

Dennis Hanson, Director
Wisconsin Training and Standards Bureau
P. O. Box 7070
Madison, WI 53707
(608) 266-8800   Fax (608) 266-7869

Donald Pierson, Executive Director
Wyoming P.O.S.T.
1710 Pacific Avenue
Cheyenne, WY 82002
(307) 358-3617   Fax (307) 358-9603

INDEX